Mariemont

A Pictorial History of a Model Town

VIEW IN THE INDUSTRIAL HOUSING SECTION · MARIEMONT · OHIO · Nov-1925 ·

Millard F. Rogers Jr.
Text

Karen Monzel Hughes
Design

Ohio University Press
Athens

Ohio University Press, Athens, Ohio 45701

ohioswallow.com

© 2011 by Ohio University Press

All rights reserved

To obtain permission to quote, reprint, or otherwise reproduce
or distribute material from Ohio University Press publications,
please contact our rights and permissions department at
(740) 593-1154 or (740) 593-4536 (fax).

Printed in China

Ohio University Press books are printed on acid-free paper ∞ ™

20 19 18 17 16 15 14 13 12 11   5 4 3 2 1

Library of Congress Cataloging-in-Publication Data

Rogers, Millard F.

 Mariemont : a pictorial history of a model town / text by Millard
F. Rogers Jr. ; design by Karen Monzel Hughes.

     p. cm.

Includes bibliographical references and index.

 ISBN 978-0-8214-1972-4 (hc : alk. paper)

1. Mariemont (Ohio)—History. 2. Mariemont (Ohio)—
History—Pictorial works. 3. New towns—Ohio—Mariemont—
History. I. Hughes, Karen Monzel. II. Title.

 F499.M295R64 2011

 977.1'77—dc22

                                          2011009368

The booklet published by the
Mariemont Company in 1925
offered tantalizing illustrations
and text to encourage potential
buyers and renters to come and
live in Mariemont, a "National
Exemplar" of town planning.

Mariemont

A Pictorial History of a Model Town

Contents

After the incorporation of the Mariemont Preservation Foundation (MPF) on December 26, 1980, one of the first archival collections received was from Warren W. Parks, chief engineer of the Mariemont Company. Part of Mr. Parks's collection consisted of over two hundred black-and-white photographs documenting the early development of Mariemont. Since then the MPF photographic collection has grown to over three thousand black-and-white and color photos.

Of significant historical value in our collection are early publications such as the 1926 *Architecture Magazine*, the Mariemont Company promotional booklet *A Descriptive and Pictured Story of Mariemont—A New Town,* and original Pathé newsreel footage taken in Mariemont during the 1930s. The MPF has the largest, most important single collection of materials pertaining to Mariemont and its founder, Mary Emery. With the acquisition of copies of the Nolen Records from Cornell University, including a copy of John Nolen's photographic scrapbook, the MPF has also become one of the largest repositories of materials on Mariemont's eminent town planner.

The MPF also has a small collection of artifacts from the Madisonville Site, a significant Late Fort Ancient archaeological site dating from AD 1450–1670 situated in Mariemont.

The archival collection of the MPF also includes well over seven thousand reference materials, including newspaper articles, early publications and promotional materials, historic maps and blueprints, broadsheets, flyers, letters, and other documents and memorabilia. Over thirty oral histories from residents have been recorded and transcribed, giving firsthand knowledge of life in Mariemont throughout the decades.

Executive Secretary and Archivist for the Mariemont Preservation Foundation, Janet Setchell has been building our archives for over twenty years. With the use of the PastPerfect museum software program, we are able to catalog, search, and retrieve information for research. Our archives are frequently utilized by professionals and students of urban planning and architecture and by other researchers of Mariemont's history.

Mariemont's rich and unique history is shared with the public through historical displays and in-school educational programs. Publications available through our bookstore include *The Mariemont Story* by Warren W. Parks and *A Dream Come True* by G. Carlton Hill Jr., documenting Mariemont's history; *Rich in Good Works,* a biography of Mary Emery, and *John Nolen and Mariemont,* both by Millard F. Rogers Jr.; as well as a DVD on Mariemont's history.

Acknowledgments

The Mariemont Preservation Foundation is grateful to the Helen G., Henry F. and Louise Teuchter Dornette Foundation and the Robert H. Reakirt Foundation for their generous financial support in the grants that made possible the development and printing of this book. They are acknowledged as follows: *This publication was assisted financially by the Helen G., Henry F. and Louise Teuchter Dornette Foundation, Fifth Third Bank, Trustee. The views expressed herein do not necessarily represent those of the Dornette Foundation, Fifth Third Bank, Trustee.*

The Robert H. Reakirt Foundation, PNC Bank, Trustee

The Mariemont Preservation Foundation gratefully acknowledges the owners of the photographs reproduced in this publication. They are listed below together with the pages where their illustrations appear. All photographs not listed below are from the archives of the Mariemont Preservation Foundation.

Pat Brand Photo: Page 98

Cincinnati Art Museum: Pages 4, 5, 20, 23, 25

Cincinnati Enquirer: Page 48

Cincinnati Historical Society: Pages 7, 21, 89, 123

Cornell University, Carl A. Kroch Library, Division of Rare and Manuscript Collections: Pages 10–14, 16–17, 26, 104

Robert Flischel: Pages 164–171

Harvard University, Peabody Museum of Archaeology & Ethnology: Pages 2, 5–7

Karen Monzel Hughes: Pages 146–163

David P. McNeill: Pages 102–103

Elizabeth Livingood McGuire: Page 25

Ron Schroeder: Pages 144–145

Lela Emery Steele: Page 22

Barbara Nolen Strong: Page 24

University of Cincinnati: Pages 22–23

The home of the Mariemont Preservation Foundation headquarters and archives is a former transformer station adjacent to Ferris House, built to house the tangle of cables, transformers, and wires bringing high-voltage electricity into the village. Designed by Richard H. Dana and graced with Palladian windows at each end and a cupola, the transformer building was donated by its owner, the Thomas J. Emery Memorial, to the Foundation and renovated for its new use in 1996–1997.

The Mariemont Preservation Foundation was incorporated in December of 1980. Its stated purpose was "to receive and maintain funds to be used for public benefit to maintain and enhance the historic integrity of the Village, to avoid urban decay and beautify the Village, and to preserve and improve parks, playgrounds and public areas. Such activities are for the ultimate purpose of enriching the lives of citizens of Mariemont."

In 2005, the Board of Trustees of the Mariemont Preservation Foundation began to discuss the need to make the extensive archive of photographs, original architects' illustrations, and other rare documents available to a wider audience. Although this treasure trove of historical articles is open to the public, the MPF is only staffed part-time and access is highly limited. The idea of creating a book took shape, and a committee was formed in early 2006. Co-chaired by Karen Monzel Hughes and Millard Rogers, the committee spent the next four years sifting through materials, developing a strategy for publication, securing grant funding, and completing the authoring and design of this book.

Author Millard F. Rogers Jr. is recognized as an authority on the genesis and planning of Mariemont and on its eminent town planner, John Nolen. He received a master's degree in art history from the University of Michigan, a doctor of humanities (honorary) degree from Xavier University, and the Gosline Fellowship for research and study at the Victoria and Albert Museum, London, with Sir John Pope-Hennessy. He is Director Emeritus of the Cincinnati Art Museum and, as a specialist in American and Spanish art, has written extensively in those fields. His books include *Randolph Rogers: American Sculptor in Rome* (1971), *Spanish Paintings in the Cincinnati Art Museum* (1978), *Sketches and Bozzetti by American Sculptors, 1800–1950* (1987), *Rich in Good Works: Mary M. Emery of Cincinnati* (2001), and *John Nolen and Mariemont: Building a New Town in Ohio* (2001). Mr. Rogers has resided in the village of Mariemont, Ohio, since 1974. An early member of the Mariemont Preservation Foundation, he served as president for many years, during which he conducted extensive research on the history of Mariemont and its predecessors and received Outstanding Citizen of Mariemont honors for his efforts. He wrote the successful nomination for Mariemont as a National Historic Landmark, awarded by the National Park Service to the village in 2007.

The book's designer, Karen Monzel Hughes, called Mariemont, Ohio, home for twenty-five years, becoming a trustee of the Mariemont Preservation Foundation in 2005. Her understanding of the importance of place-making stems from the firsthand experience of living in Mariemont, leading to the design of an award-winning interactive CD-ROM, *Seaside: A Town by Design*, documenting the architecturally significant Seaside, Florida, a town based on the planning principles of John Nolen. As a member of Mariemont's fiftieth anniversary planning committee, she designed the bronze fountain that now stands at the center of Mariemont Square. Currently serving as Associate Dean in the College of Design, Architecture, Art, and Planning at the University of Cincinnati, and Associate Professor of Design, she received her BS in Graphic Design and MA in Communication Arts from the University of Cincinnati.

Janet Setchell has served as secretary for the Mariemont Preservation Foundation since 1986, and was absolutely invaluable to this effort. Her knowledge of the extensive archives provided the foundation of the book's contents. She spent countless hours poring over documents and scanning them digitally. This book would not have been possible without her devotion to building, cataloging, and maintaining the MPF archives.

Amy Fischer and Pam Pfeifer Gaines provided the support needed to assure completion of the project. They researched grant opportunities and publishers and assisted with the selection of the final documents for inclusion. Amy wrote grant applications that resulted in funding through the Reakirt and Dornette Foundations.

Students at the University of Cincinnati's College of Design, Architecture, Art, and Planning provided design and production support: Lisa Bambach, Graphic Design; Ryan Evans, Graphic Design; and Jacob Fox, Digital Design. Kim Simmons provided invaluable support in photographing original drawings.

A Short History of Mariemont

Today's visitor to Mariemont (pronounced MERRY-mont) encounters what appears to be a community from another place and time, perhaps a country village in England's Cotswold region. A stone church with ancient roof that dates from 1300 abuts an aged graveyard. Tree-lined streets pass through neighborhoods rich in Tudor-style half-timber and stucco-decorated residences. Red brick with crisp white wooden trim identifies Georgian-style buildings. A grassy median and woods lure the visitor along the main road through Mariemont and into a spacious town square with gardens and fountain, bordered by shops, an inn, an ice cream parlor, restaurants, and woods. Straying deeper into this very walkable community, the visitor finds parklands, soccer and baseball fields, a swim club, and a magnificent carillon, among other amenities. The village's character is determined by its well-settled, welcoming appearance.

Mariemont was the vision of its founder, Mary Muhlenberg Emery (1844–1927). A philanthropist who supported many causes, she sought to alleviate housing problems in Cincinnati and establish a model for future planned communities in America. The preeminent town planner in the United States, John Nolen (1869–1937), was retained in 1920 to design a new town, which would be built on farmland only ten miles east of downtown Cincinnati. With silver spade in hand, Mrs. Emery broke ground on April 23, 1923, in front of the historic Ferris House. Her representative, Charles J. Livingood (1866–1952), served as director of the private Mariemont project from its inception and during its development.

Mariemont was intended to be a well-planned and nearly self-sufficient town that would provide modestly priced rental apartments and town houses, architect-designed single-family homes, and a wide range of commercial, recreational, and educational structures. Mariemont followed the English Garden City prototype, particularly the models of Letchworth, Port Sunlight, and Hampstead Garden Suburb, as well as Forest Hills Gardens in New York City. Nolen determined the footprint of Mariemont, its radial street pattern surrounding the town square, and the complete layout for streets, lot lines, and landscape and park features.

John Nolen's plan of 1921 labeled the community of 253 acres "A National Exemplar," suggesting a future role for Mariemont. Nationally recognized architects for the residential and commercial buildings were selected from New York, Boston, Philadelphia, and Cincinnati. Equally famous as a landscape architect, Nolen provided the original design and planting scheme for parks, streets, and homes.

The Mariemont Company, formed by Mrs. Emery to construct the village, was dissolved in 1931, and its assets were turned over to the Thomas J. Emery Memorial. This private foundation supervised the village until 1941, when Mariemont was incorporated under Ohio law. The Village of Mariemont now covers 650 acres and has a population of 3,300 (U.S. Census, 2000). It maintains a highly ranked public school system, has easy access to a large city and its cultural and commercial offerings, and possesses a high degree of integrity in its plan and architecture. In 2007, Mariemont was awarded National Historic Landmark status by the U.S. government.

Face jar, Fort Ancient Culture,
ca. AD 1450–1600.
Peabody Museum of
Archaelogy & Ethnology,
Harvard University

Earliest Residents: Prehistoric to 1800

A small corner of today's Mariemont once was the center of a relatively large Native American settlement by the Fort Ancient people. From about 1450 to 1670, their community of two to three hundred people dwelt on a high ridge overlooking the Little Miami River. Farmers who grew corn, they are considered the first agriculturists in the Ohio Valley.

This important example of Fort Ancient culture in Mariemont is called the Madisonville Site, named for its proximity to the community nearest to present-day Mariemont.

Archeological explorations of the site were first carried out in 1878 by Dr. Charles L. Metz (1847–1926), a well-known physician with an office and home in Madisonville. Under his supervision, a corps of amateur diggers dug and opened many pits, revealing burial sites, storage bins, and remains of dwellings. Metz's efforts attracted Harvard University Professor Frederick W. Putnam, who led professional archeologists in excavating the site between 1882 and 1911.

The last occupants of the Madisonville Site probably were the Shawnee Tribe, who had some contact with colonial settlements and traders. Like the prehistoric residents, the Shawnees were gone when the Mariemont area was first settled following passage of the Northwest Ordinance in 1787.

Dr. Charles L. Metz, amateur archeologist and student of prehistoric Native American culture, initiated exploration of the Madisonville Site in the late nineteenth century.

Pedestal jar, Fort Ancient culture, ca. AD 1450–1600.

The Madisonville Site in Mariemont was the home of Native Americans, a lively community high on a bluff above the Little Miami River. Living there from the fifteenth to the seventeenth centuries, the residents were primarily growers of corn and gatherers and augmented their food supply by hunting. During excavations, many skillfully made clay vessels and objects using animal decoration or figures were found in burials. Without any painted decoration, the clay objects were fired in ground pits, producing the characteristic black surface finish. *Peabody Museum of Archaelogy & Ethnology, Harvard University*

Animal forms modestly decorated the vessels from the Madisonville Site, as this Salamander pot, a major example of the craftsmanship and ingenuity of Fort Ancient artists, indicates.

1800

1900

1910

1920

1930

1940

6

Laborers hired by Dr. Metz uncovered burials, storage pits, and remnants of communal houses in their search for artifacts of the long-disappeared Fort Ancient people at the Madisonville Site. After Dr. Metz's early efforts, Harvard University's professional archeologists undertook work at the site into the twentieth century.

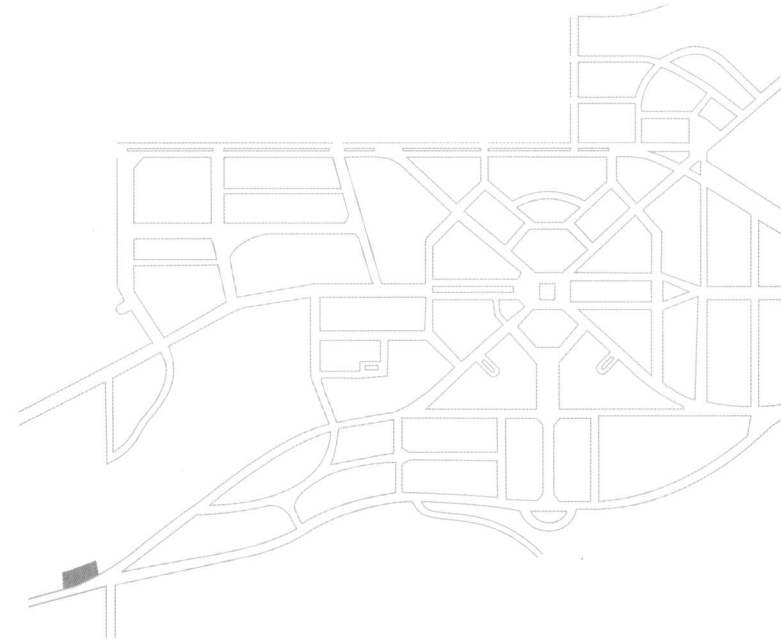

Settlement and Farms: 1800-1910

Fields and Orchards

Settlements began in earnest after 1787, when the Northwest Ordinance opened vast areas for land acquisition in present-day Ohio, Michigan, Wisconsin, Indiana, and Illinois. A large tract in southwest Ohio, known as the Miami Purchase, was acquired by John Cleves Symmes, a speculator from New Jersey. He sold 640 acres to the earliest settlers in the region: the Stites, Ferris, Peck, Knapp, and Lockwood families. The land these families purchased, where Mariemont stands today, was once covered with dense woods and untilled fields.

Throughout the nineteenth century and into the twentieth, about three hundred acres that eventually would be the core of Mariemont became farmland. Cornfields and orchards dotted the landscape by the 1850s. Although close to downtown Cincinnati along a federal highway (U.S. 50), and in spite of the encroachment of nearby towns to the west and to the north, all of the acreage eventually purchased by Mary Emery for her planned town was rural and agricultural.

Among the simple farmhouses and barns scattered in the fields and along the narrow roads in the acreage that would become Mariemont was the Ferris House. One of the original settlers, Eliphalet Ferris (1774–1859), built this brick home beginning in 1802 and continued making additions until about 1812. The Federal-style building is thought to be the oldest brick house still standing on its original site in Hamilton County. By 1921, it served as the field headquarters for the construction of Mariemont and had a triangulation station for surveys mounted on its roof.

Fields and Orchards

The Ferris Cemetery

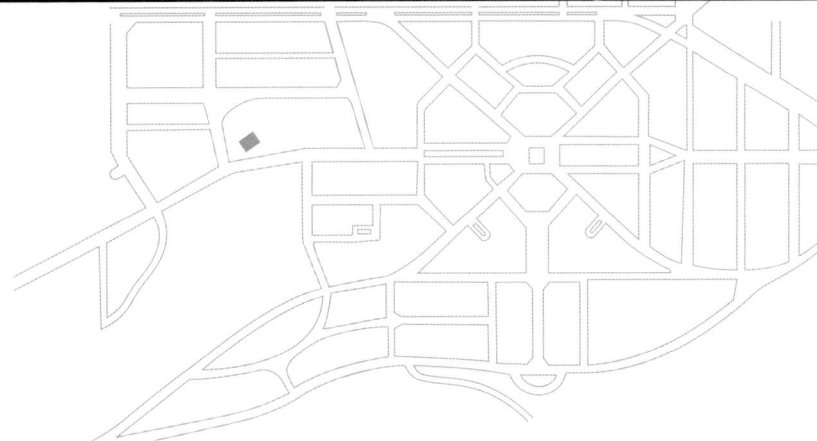

Obelisks and other gravestones mark burials in Mariemont's pioneer cemetery, begun in the 1820s.

A group of photographs taken in June 1922 by John Nolen's associate, Philip W. Foster, illustrates the pastoral appearance of the landscape of rolling fields and woods on which Nolen's plan would develop.

General View

Fields and Orchards

The great sweep of open fields and the cornstalks where the town square was to be placed in Nolen's plan is a dramatic record of the eventual center of the village. By May 1922, Nolen drafted a change in the location of Wooster Pike so that it followed an easterly course in direct line with the highway as it entered the town square from the west.

Site for TOWN CENTER from Wooster Pike

Intersection Wooster Pike and Plainville Pike

Seeds of an Idea: 1910-1921

The Village of Mariemont was designed in the first quarter of the twentieth century by the eminent American town planner John Nolen for its founder, Mary Muhlenberg Emery, and the Mariemont Company she formed. As the widow of the wealthy industrialist and real estate developer Thomas J. Emery (1830–1906), Mary Emery became Cincinnati's most noted and generous philanthropist. She was particularly devoted to social welfare, cultural, and educational causes.

In an album of black-and-white photographs taken by John Nolen in 1922, he carefully noted on each one the few roads or landmarks identifying the agricultural acres that soon would become Mariemont. Nolen's plan was developed by this date, and many locations pinpointed on the plan are indicated in the fields by large wooden signs heralding what was to come.

Mrs. Emery's vision for Mariemont was to create a new town that would be professionally designed, provide quality housing at affordable rents, and offer building lots and houses for sale to individual builder-owners. With its shops and amenities within a suburban setting near a major city, the community was to be self-supporting and nearly self-sufficient. Mariemont was to offer green spaces and parks, a fully built infrastructure, and clean air in a setting away from city smoke. Like other philanthropists of her day, Mary Emery hoped to ease a critical social need and set an example that could be developed in other locations of the United States.

With the help of Charles J. Livingood, a trusted employee of Thomas Emery's Sons and a surrogate son of Thomas and Mary Emery, the wealthy widow embarked on her most costly benefaction. Livingood began the study of European and American planned communities from 1910 to 1913. Seeking models, Livingood was particularly impressed with the English Garden City movement and the examples of Letchworth, Port Sunlight, and Hampstead Garden Suburb.

A spread of 253 acres owned by about thirty parties in Columbia Township, an unincorporated area, was purchased beginning in 1915 and surveyed in 1918. The final acquisition of land was made in 1922. John Nolen would have a clean slate on which to execute his design.

Site for VILLAGE GREEN (woods at right)

MARIEMONT TOWN CENTER

Mary M. Emery, John Nolen, Charles J. Livingood

Founder, Town Planner, Project Director

Born in New York City, Mary Muhlenberg Hopkins moved with her family to Cincinnati as a youngster. In 1866 she married the city's most eligible bachelor, Thomas J. Emery, the principal partner in a Cincinnati enterprise, Thomas Emery's Sons, that created its wealth initially from lard oil and candles and later from extensive real estate holdings across the nation. Their two sons, Sheldon and Albert, predeceased both parents, and by age sixty-two she was a widow and the major beneficiary of her husband's large fortune. Among Mary Emery's many philanthropic efforts after her husband's death, certainly the most costly was the creation of Mariemont. She was its only financial backer.

"Mariemont," Rhode Island, home of Mary M. and Thomas J. Emery, designed by architect Richard Morris Hunt, 1871. Summer residence of the Emerys, the sixty-acre estate was renowned for its gardens and vistas to the sea, planned by the eminent American firm of landscape architects Olmsted Brothers.

John Nolen was commissioned in 1920 to design Mariemont. Born and reared in Philadelphia, he graduated from the University of Pennsylvania in 1893. After completing his master's degree in landscape architecture at Harvard University in 1903, he established his practice in that field in Cambridge, Massachusetts, and was soon engaged in town planning. Between 1905 and 1935, Nolen was probably the busiest planner in America, working on some 450 projects. He was a popular lecturer on town planning and landscape architecture, as well as the author of many books and articles. He held prestigious posts in professional organizations, all the while providing plans for both nascent towns and established cities needing transformation. Nolen is considered one of the founders of the American planning profession.

Charles Jacob Livingood was born in Reading, Pennsylvania, the son of a lawyer and real estate developer. At Harvard University, his classmate was the Emerys' oldest son, Sheldon. Their friendship led to Livingood's long association with the Emery family. In 1890 he accepted employment with Thomas Emery's Sons and moved to Cincinnati. After the death of her husband in 1906, Mary Emery sought the counsel of many advisors. None was as close as Livingood, who served throughout her widowhood as secretary and manager of her business affairs and philanthropies. Mariemont's design, construction, and management was his principal assignment in his lifetime.

Mary M. Emery.
Portrait miniature
by Effie C. Trader, 1908.

"Edgecliffe," Cincinnati
residence of Mary M. and
Thomas J. Emery, a rusticated
stone mansion of thirty-one
rooms in East Walnut Hills,
commanded a spectacular
view of the Ohio River. Now
demolished, it was designed by
Cincinnati architect Samuel
Hannaford in 1881.

The two sons of Mary M. and Thomas J. Emery, Albert (1868-1884) at left and Sheldon (1867-1890). The older son was a classmate of Charles J. Livingood at Harvard University, and this friendship led later to Livingood's involvement as Mary Emery's secretary, manager, and surrogate son. Both Emery children would be memorialized with streets named for them in Mariemont.

Dixie Selden, Mrs. Thomas J. Emery, 1921, oil on canvas.

B. L. Pruitt, Thomas J. Emery, bronze sculpture.

Thomas J. Emery and Mary Muhlenberg Hopkins were married in Cincinnati in 1866. The city's most eligible bachelor, and certainly one of the wealthiest, Thomas was a partner with his brothers John J. and J. Howard in the very successful real estate and lard oil business started by their father. The business empire, Thomas Emery's Sons, grew to include real estate holdings across the nation, including land and buildings in San Francisco, Denver, New York City, and Cincinnati.

Portrait of Thomas J. Emery by Emil Fuchs.

When John Nolen was contacted in the autumn of 1920 for the Mariemont commission, he was at the forefront of town planning in America. An early project, a comprehensive plan for San Diego (1908), led to designs for many new towns, such as Myers Park (1911) in North Carolina; Overlook Colony (1917) in Delaware; Union Park Gardens (1918) in Delaware; Kingsport, Tennessee (1916–19); and two villages in Florida, Belleair (1924) and Venice (1925).

John Nolen, ca. 1926.

Charles J. Livingood entered employment with Thomas Emery's Sons in 1890. After the death of Thomas J. Emery in 1906, Mary Emery contemplated several projects that she felt would improve housing in Cincinnati. With Livingood's urging, she agreed that the English Garden City model was appropriate for a planned community that she would finance. He was assigned the responsibility of realizing this vision.

Charles J. Livingood, ca. 1890

Portrait of Charles J. Livingood by Fritz Werner, 1941.

John Nolen and His Plan: 1921-1925

National Exemplar of Town Planning

Nolen produced his master plan for Mariemont, Ohio, by July 1921 and labeled it, in large, block letters, MARIEMONT—A NEW TOWN. The layout also bore the prophetic subtitle "An Interpretation of Modern City Planning Principles Applied to a Small Community to produce local Happiness. A National Exemplar." The new town's name, Mariemont, derived from Mary and Thomas Emery's estate at Middletown, Rhode Island, a suburb of Newport. An extended plan was made in 1925 by Nolen when Mrs. Emery acquired additional land for residences and an industrial section, called Westover.

Nolen was charged in the autumn of 1920 with planning a new town that would employ his well-known design skills. Although not a utopian community, Mariemont was intended to ease a social need for better housing and to set an example that could be developed in other locations across the United States.

MARIEMONT
CINCINNATI DISTRICT, OHIO
STATISTICAL STATEMENT
DATA HEREWITH IS BASED ON A TOTAL OF 253.58 ACRES

LOTS	ACREAGES		PERCENTAGES		LOTS
HOUSES	111.52		43.97		**Number of House Lots**
STORES & APARTMENTS	10.04		3.97		**759**
Total		121.56		47.94	Houses per net acre
SEMI-PUBLIC PROPERTIES					**6.81**
GARAGE	.89		.35		
FILLING STATION	.07		.03		Average Lot Area
HOTEL	.87		.34		**.15 acres**
BANK	.37		.15		
CHURCH	.55		.22		Normal Lot Sizes
CHURCH & CEMETERY	1.00		.39		Detached
CHURCH	.76		.30		50 ft. × 120 ft.
Total		4.51		1.78	80 ft. × 120 ft.
PUBLIC PROPERTIES					Semi-Detached
POST OFFICE	.83		.33		30 ft. × 100 ft.
TOWN HALL	1.88		.74		Group
FIRE STATION	.32		.13		20 ft. × 100 ft.
PUBLIC MARKET	1.19		.47		
LIBRARY	.97		.36		Northwest Section
COMMUNITY BUILDINGS	2.57		1.01		Density per net acre
SCHOOL & STADIUM	8.59		3.37		**11.09**
SCHOOL	1.00		.39		
PARKS & PLAYGROUNDS	51.76		20.45		
Total		69.11		27.25	
STREETS					**LENGTH OF STREETS**
FORTY FOOT	10.00		3.95		40' WIDE 2.2 MILES
FIFTY FOOT	22.84		9.02		50' " 3.7 "
SIXTY FOOT	12.39		4.87		60' " 1.7 "
EIGHTY FOOT CARLINE	8.01		3.15		80' " .7 "
150 FOOT SPECIAL	5.16		2.04		150' " .3 "
Total		58.40		23.03	Total 8.6 MILES
TOTAL	253.58	253.58	100.00	100.00	

One of the first documents submitted by John Nolen with his 1921 plan was a statistical statement noting the land assignments within approximately 253 acres comprising the original area acquired by the Mariemont Company. Present-day Mariemont covers about 650 acres, primarily due to additional purchases made by Mrs. Emery.

Nolen's first visit to Mariemont's site was on November 29, 1920, when he walked the cornfields and surveyed the property. With pencil and pad, he scribbled notes and dimensions, labeling the pages with the title "Mariemont," probably the first use of this name.

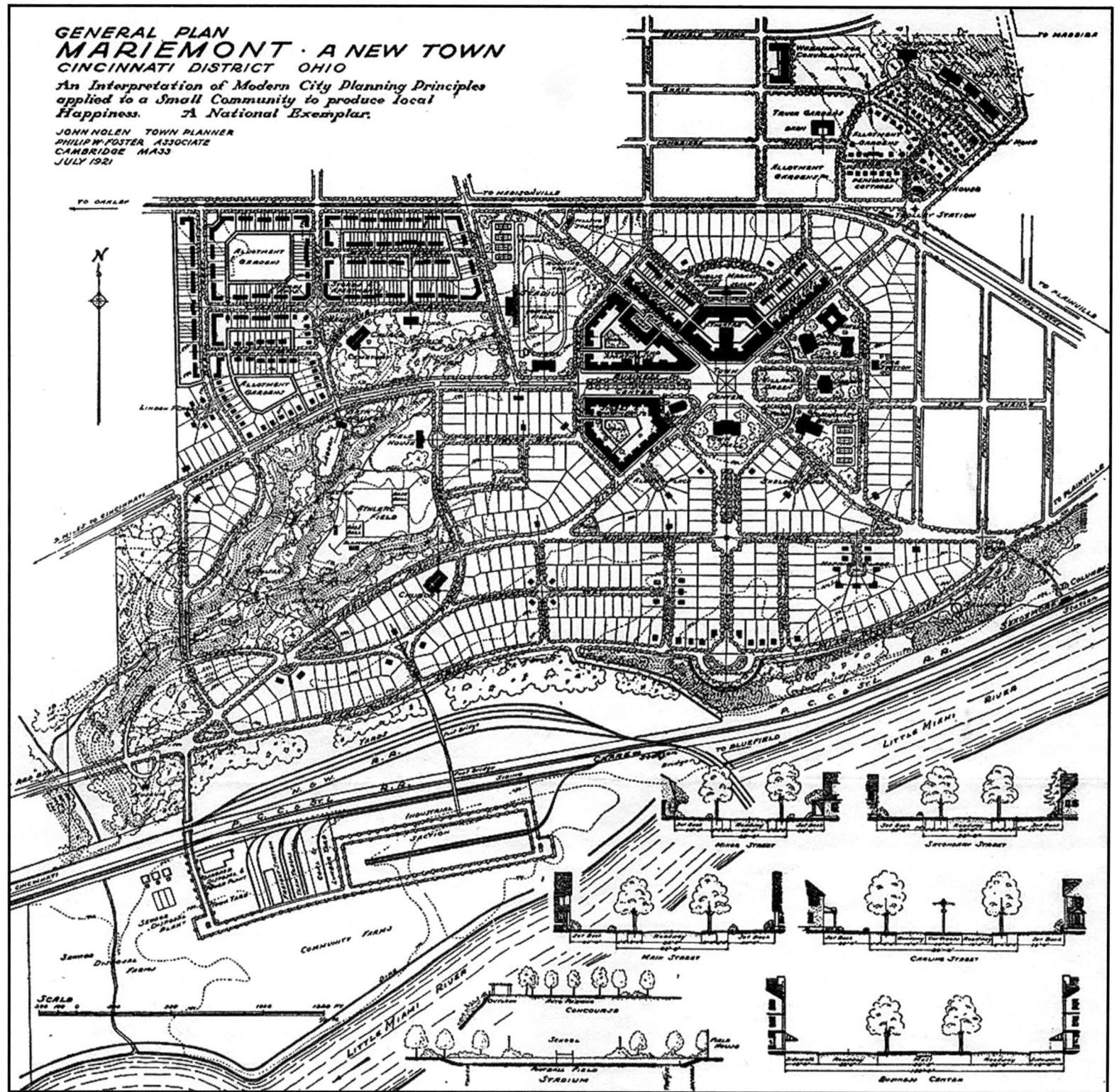

GENERAL PLAN
MARIEMONT · A NEW TOWN
CINCINNATI DISTRICT OHIO
An Interpretation of Modern City Planning Principles
applied to a Small Community to produce Local
Happiness.   A National Exemplar.
JOHN NOLEN   TOWN PLANNER
PHILIP W. FOSTER ASSOCIATE
CAMBRIDGE MASS
JULY 1921

The original plan for
Mariemont, dated July 1921,
provided the framework for
all streets, lot lines, parks, and
proposed buildings. The plan
was titled auspiciously "General
Plan, Mariemont, A New Town,
Cincinnati District, Ohio, An
Interpretation of Modern City
Planning Principles Applied
to a Small Community to
Promote Local Happiness.
A National Exemplar." Due
to Mary Emery's death in
1927 and national economic
failures beginning in 1929,
some assigned buildings, the
industrial section as assigned
originally, and certain
structures were never built as
drawn in Nolen's master design.

National Exemplar of Town Planning

Following discussions with Charles J. Livingood in 1921–22, Nolen rendered several watercolors to illustrate ideas for the town square and its buildings, the Resthaven complex planned for retirement of Emery estate pensioners, including the hospital, and cottages. The buildings designed by architects commissioned a few years later bear an uncanny resemblance to those visionary watercolors by Nolen.

MARIEMONT · TOWN CENTER
JOHN NOLEN TOWN PLANNER CAMBRIDGE MASS

1800 1900 1910 1920 **1921** 1925 1930 1940

MARIEMONT

SKETCH FOR FARM BUILDINGS

John Nolen, Town Planner
Philip W. Foster, Associate

·VIEW·OF·THE·TOWN·HALL·AND·BANK·MARIEMONT·OHIO·

Drawn but Never Built: 1921-1925

Envisioned Buildings

Just as some major town plans and construction projects fail today because the ideas behind them are too lofty, money is too scarce, or the concept fades, Mariemont fell short of seeing all the structures developed that had been envisioned. After Nolen charted his plan in 1921, drawings of imagined buildings were commissioned for a library, a post office, a massive three-story arcade and theater block, and a Palladian-style town hall. Beautifully drafted by Boston architect Hubert G. Ripley in 1922, in some cases clearly for publicity purposes, these grandiose structures were never blueprinted nor built. Such buildings were impressive in scale and purpose but grandiose beyond Livingood's ideas for recreating an English country village.

Some planned but never built structures by the Mariemont Company included a long bridge over Whiskey Creek, a fieldhouse, and pensioners' cottages for retirees in Emery employment. The twenty architects who were commissioned produced detailed drawings for assigned construction sites, but only thirteen of the twenty had their designs executed in the new town. The others failed for various reasons but remain as unfulfilled ideas in the original vision.

Hubert Ripley was a talented architect and draftsman working in his Boston office with his partner, Addison LeBoutillier. Before they were given a commission for two apartment buildings and a group of town houses, Ripley produced a set of four drawings in charcoal and pencil to delineate buildings and locations suggested by Livingood. His facile drawings suggested buildings on a grand scale: a town hall, bank, corner of a residential street, and portions of the town square. Livingood liked the "bold, free manner" of the drawings but groused that they were not following his concept of creating the character of an English country village.

Envisioned Buildings

A·VIEW·IN·THE·RESIDENCE·SECTION · *MARIEMONT* ·OHIO   NOV-1922

Beginning in 1922, nearly fifty architects or firms were considered for commissions by Livingood and Nolen, all of them from Boston, Cincinnati, New York, or Philadelphia. Some architects, such as Allen W. Jackson of Boston, were assigned a location for "brick and stucco cottages designed to show the character of housing that will prevail in the higher priced sections of Mariemont," as determined by Livingood. Jackson drafted detailed elevations, but his commission never was fulfilled.

Hubert Ripley produced this imagined view, dated November 1922.

A. W. JACKSON, Boston, Mass., Architect

Envisioned Buildings

VIEW IN THE INDUSTRIAL HOUSING SECTION· ·MARIEMONT· OHIO· NOV·1922·

Drawings by Hubert Ripley placed the Mariemont Community Church nestled among town houses and a storefront; another drawing suggests the town square bounded by a three-story structure that was never built. Although not resembling exactly what eventually emerged at these sites, Ripley's drawings imagined what might arise on Nolen's plan.

A · VIEW · OF · THE · TOWN · CENTER · MARIEMONT · OHIO ·

Envisioned Buildings

Planned as the principal structure in the village was a massive three-story block of shops, offices, and apartments bordering the town square on its north side between Miami Road and Madisonville Road. Designed by the Cincinnati architectural firm of Joseph Steinkamp and Brother with half-timber, stucco, gables, and steeply pitched roof in the Tudor Revival style, it echoes the famous Rows in Chester, England. Handsome as it is, the building was beyond what the Mariemont Company wished to build.

This imposing elevation, showing the c
of the Town Center. Under the long arca
cade, with shops, leading back to the the
  Here will be located the larger retail st
insure fresh air and sunshine the structu
  Ample space has been provided for the
only in part depicted.

THE THEATRE BLOCK
Mariemont Town Center

Jos. G. Steinkamp & Bro., Cincinnati, Oh
Architec
Paul P. Cret, Philadelphia, P
Consulta

ral portion of the principal structure in the village, gives the key-note to the architectural scheme

l sidewalk will pass the busy life of the commercial district, for in addition, there will be an Ar-

s, with a variety of offices, a lodge room and numerous small apartments in the upper stories. To

shallow and in the rear gives upon spacious open courts.

ural extension of other business blocks to the right and left of this central building which is here

Groundbreaking for the New Town: 1923

Among the many philanthropies of Mary Emery, her vision for a new town was most closely related to the real estate programs of her late husband and her brother-in-law. But her sympathetic interest in establishing a community that would blend rental housing of good quality with privately owned single-family dwellings was her most costly financial venture. Records indicate that Mrs. Emery invested seven million dollars in land acquisition and construction of Mariemont between 1910 and 1927.

Holding a bouquet of roses in one hand and a silver spade in the other, Mary Emery led the groundbreaking ceremony for Mariemont on April 23, 1923, on the lawn in front of Ferris House. The founder and patron of Mariemont was surrounded by over a hundred friends, advisors, construction workers, and their families, including a few children who shared the event that officially launched the new town. Among the distinguished guests were Mrs. Emery's pastor, the Reverend Frank H. Nelson, and Thomas Hogan Jr. and John Schindel, officers of the Mariemont Company. But absent were John Nolen and Charles J. Livingood.

The groundbreaking not only marked the official beginning of Mariemont, but also celebrated the first anniversary of the project's announcement. Cincinnati newspapers reported extravagantly on the event, heralding Mariemont as "the cynosure of all sociological eyes . . . a great experiment . . . born of a silver spade in its mouth . . . its future seems assured."

Memorials to Mariemont's founder, town planner, and project director occur throughout the village, such as the inscribed monument at the east end of the town square, erected in 1955 by the Thomas J. Emery Memorial trustees.

The Ceremonial Birth of Mariemont

A festive event, the official ceremony in April 1923 was captured in this panoramic photograph. A three-foot shaft of granite placed in front of the founder was later inserted in the ground at the exact spot where the silver spade inaugurated the Mariemont project.

1800   1900   1910   1920   1923   1930   1940

Architects and Their Buildings: 1923-1930

With Nolen's plan in hand by July 1921, the selection of architects could begin. Seeking advice from John Nolen, Charles J. Livingood visualized Mariemont as derived primarily from English models, especially the English Garden City towns of Letchworth, Port Sunlight, and Hampstead Garden Suburb and America's Forest Hills Gardens. Architects were picked who could embrace the vision and work in revival styles.

These men and women were well versed in reviving conservative Norman-Gothic, Tudor, Jacobean, and Georgian architectural styles. Buildings on Mariemont's plan were to connote stability and character and give ready recognition in established neighborhoods along winding streets and in cul-de-sacs. Modernism, Bauhaus, and Frank Lloyd Wright influences and styles were never considered as choices.

Beginning in 1922, Livingood and Nolen visited architects in their studios and offices and discussed their accomplishments. Lists of candidates were drawn up and architects were commissioned from only four cities: New York, Boston, Philadelphia, and Cincinnati. Final selection rested with Livingood. Each architect was assigned a particular location in Nolen's plan. Commissions were given for a group of buildings (group housing, apartments, town houses, etc.) or individual buildings (Mariemont Community Church, Dale Park School, etc.). Initially, the largest concentration of residential housing occurred in the northwest section of Mariemont, where rental units were planned to adjoin shops, an elementary school, a recreation center, and a church.

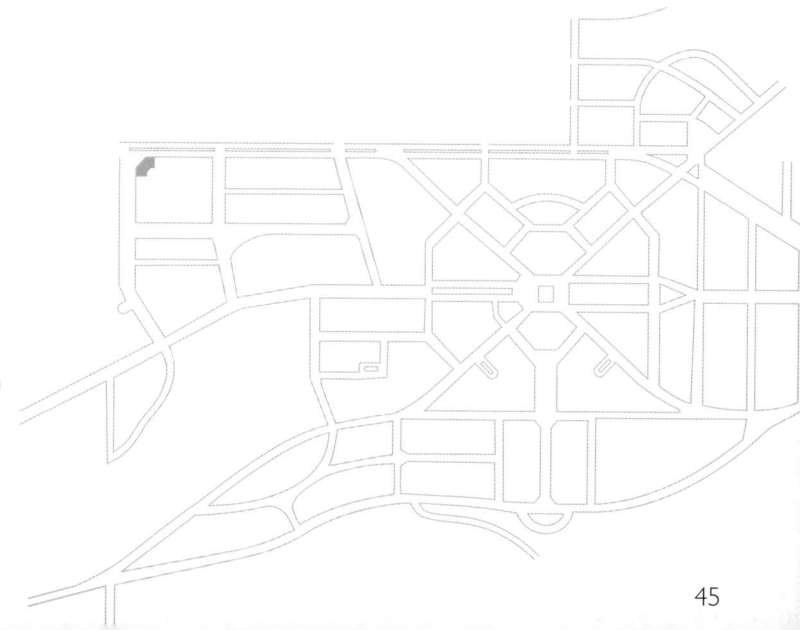

The MacKenzie Apartments at the northwest corner of Mariemont were built in 1924 and designed by Clinton MacKenzie, a New York City architect who had a close association with Nolen in the latter's design of Kingsport, Tennessee. MacKenzie was chosen by Livingood and Nolen "because of his countrywide reputation in constructing reasonably priced group housing." The building was the largest residential building except for the Ripley and LeBoutillier buildings a few blocks away.

Earliest Construction and Styles

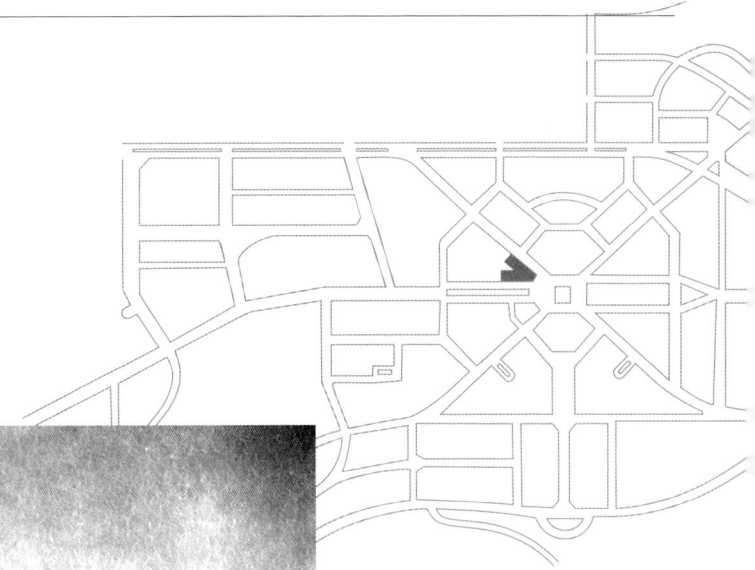

This view of the Mariemont Inn was taken by a nationally recognized photographer, Nancy Ford Cones, who was commissioned in 1926 by the Mariemont Company to record the young community of Mariemont. Designed by the Cincinnati architectural firm of Zettel and Rapp, the Inn was planned as a V-shaped, Tudor Revival structure stretching a block in each direction along two roads that intersected the town square. Construction began in 1925, but the Inn as built was only half its intended size.

1800   1900   1910   1920   1923   1930   1940

The Inn
MARIEMONT. OHIO

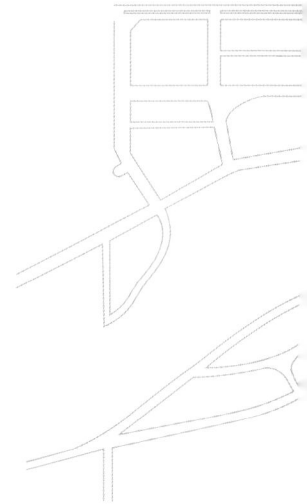

High on a hill overlooking the village, the Mariemont Hospital, part of Resthaven's complex, was intended to serve village residents as well as surrounding communities. It was designed by the prestigious Cincinnati firm of Samuel Hannaford and Sons. Expectations exceeded accomplishment with the hospital, which was not fully operational until 1942. One of several buildings in Mariemont capped by a decorative cupola, the building now serves as a retirement and nursing facility.

1800   1900   1910   1920   1923   1930   1940

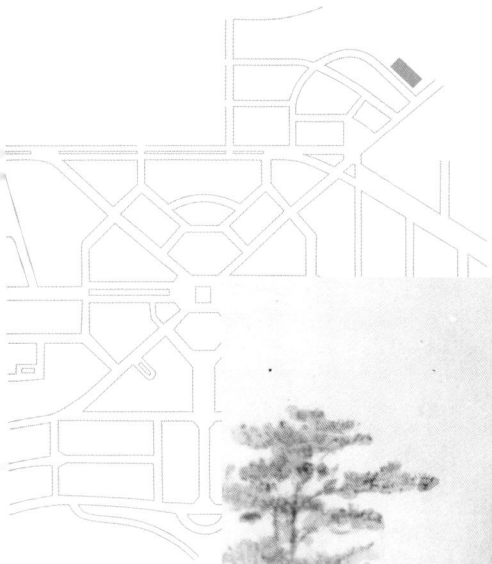

The
Hospital Group
Mariemont Ohio
Samuel Hannaford & Sons Archts

This rendering of houses on Sheldon Close suggested to prospective developers the preferred Tudor Revival style of architecture for residences in Mariemont. Named for Sheldon Emery, the deceased older son of Mary and Thomas J. Emery, the ten units built in 1925 around a grassy close became the final construction project for residences by the Mariemont Company. The architect, Grosvenor Atterbury of New York, was highly regarded nationally. His reputation and experience as the architect of Forest Hills Gardens, New York, a 1909 forerunner to Mariemont, won him the contract to design this neighborhood setting. Atterbury, was educated at Yale University and received his architecture degree from Columbia University. He then worked for the prestigious firm of McKim, Mead and White, where he apprenticed under Stanford White.

GROSVENOR·ATTERBURY·ARCHITECT
STOWE·PHELPS·&·JOHN·TOMPKINS·Assoc

·SHELDON·CLOSE·MADISONVILLE·ROAD·VILLAGE·OF·MARIEMONT·CINCINNATI·OHIO·

1800   1900   1910   1920   1923   1930   1940

50

Construction of Sheldon Close houses (one of the finished "bookend" houses is shown in this photograph by Nancy Ford Cones) closely followed Atterbury's rendering, which attempted to replicate the quaintness of English cottages from the Cotswolds of England.

Albert Place was named for
Albert, the younger son of
Thomas and Mary Emery. The
whitewashed brick houses echo
those in Letchworth, England,
a precursor town designed
twenty years earlier. Designed
by Philadelphia architect,
Robert R. McGoodwin, and
begun in 1923, Albert Place
was the first of four pocket
satellites intended to anchor
Mariemont neighborhoods.
The architect's plan designates
the lane that ran behind
the houses, insisted on by
McGoodwin to keep services
and automobile parking away
from the grassy center of
Albert Place.

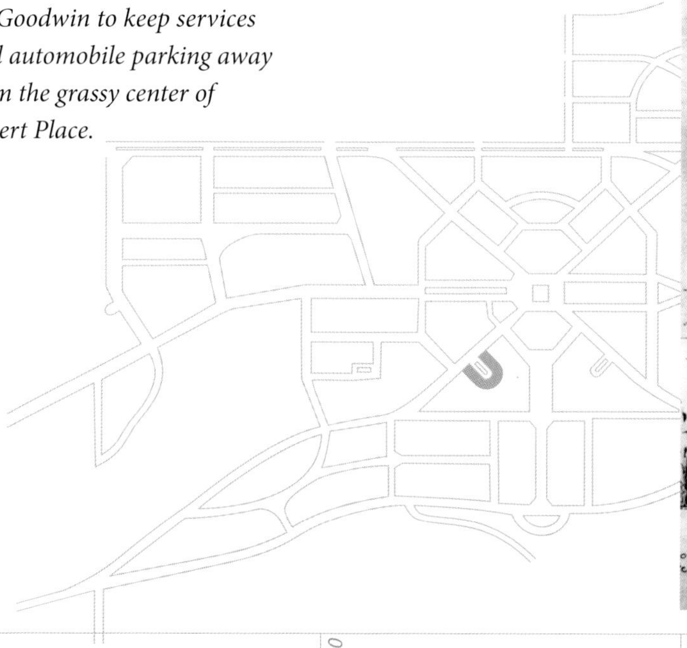

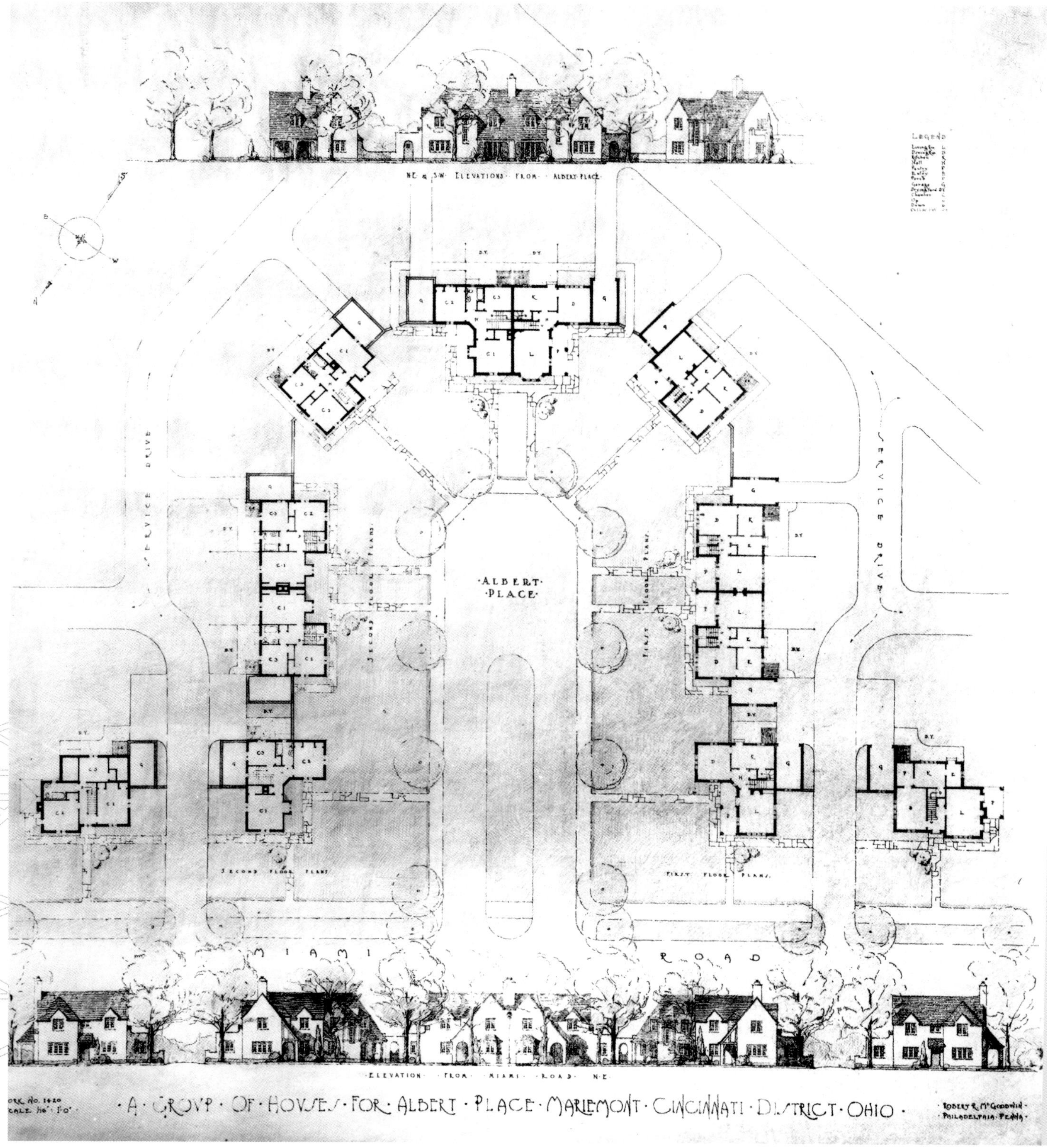

A · GROVP · OF · HOVSES · FOR · ALBERT · PLACE · MARIEMONT · CINCINNATI · DISTRICT · OHIO

Earliest Construction and Styles

AEROPLANE VIEW
OF
DENNY PLACE
MARIEMONT   OHIO

Lois L. Howe & Manning Architects
Boston Mass

1800   1900   1910   1920   1923   1930   1940

In the first decades of the twentieth century, there were only a few architectural firms headed by women. One of these rarities was the Boston studio of Lois L. Howe and Eleanor Manning. Their firm specialized in designs for private residences and was well known to Nolen. The women architects were commissioned in 1922, producing designs for Denny Place in a refined Tudor Revival style that employed native fieldstone and stucco. Named for Mary Emery's mother, Denny Place captures some of the character of Blaise Hamlet, an eighteenth-century group of cottages that was one of the first planned communities in England.

SEPT. 4 · 1925

1950   1960   1970   1980   1990   2000

55

Earliest Construction and Styles

OAK·ST, ELM § CHESTNUT·STREETS
~ MARIEMONT ~

C·W·SHORT·JR· ARCHITECT
CINCINNATI · NEW YORK · LONDON

SCALE OF PLANS

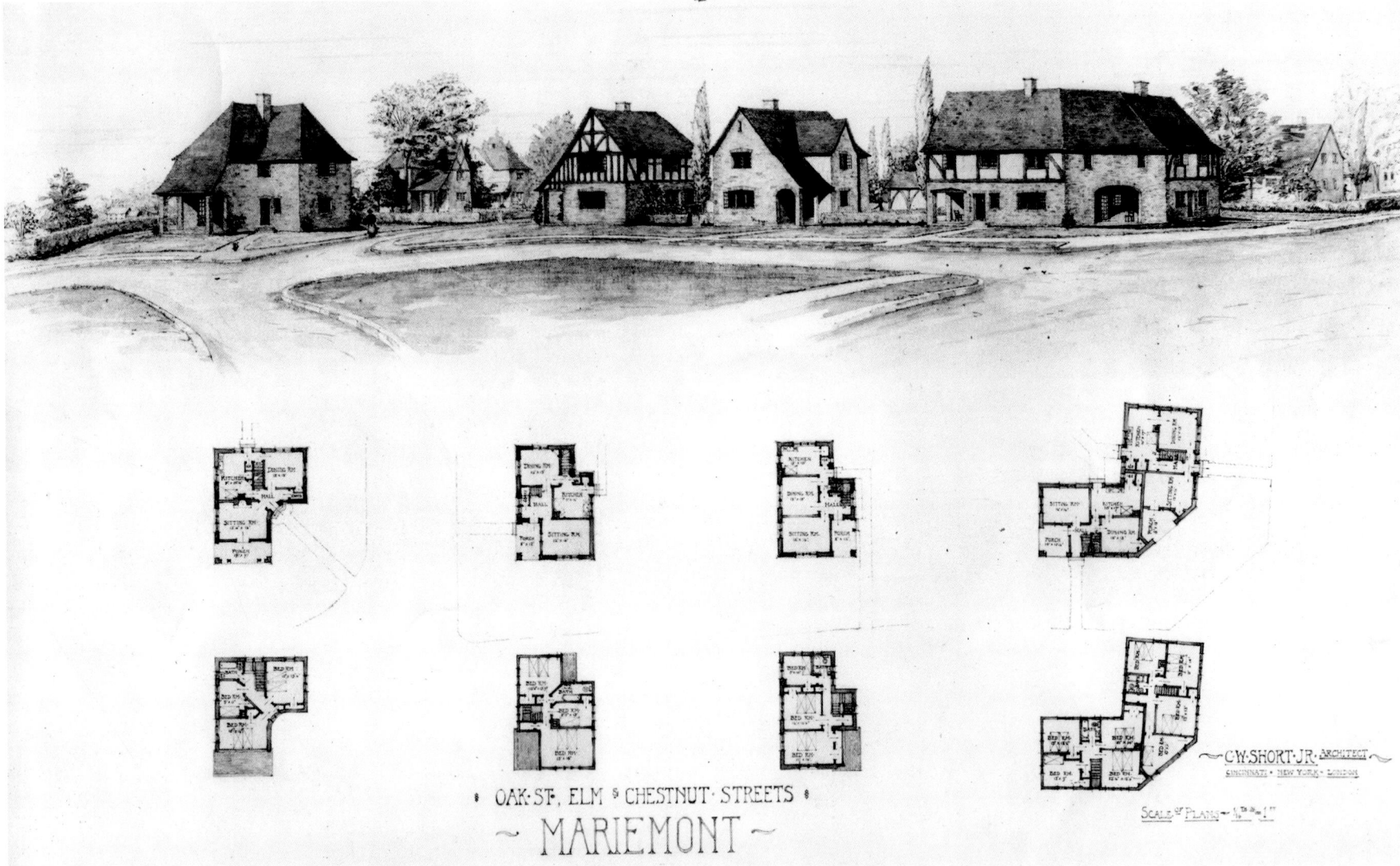

A group of "Small English houses," as they were called when built, was planned by Cincinnati architect and ardent Anglophile, Charles W. Short, in 1924. The residences overlook the Mariemont Community Church and its surrounding green space. Deeply recessed windows and curiously flaring roofs, are unique elements in the half-timber, stone, and stucco exteriors.

16-28-24.

Earliest Construction and Styles

JULY 3, 1925

In 1924, the well-known Cincinnati architectural firm of Elzner and Anderson designed a group of two-story frame bungalows stretching along Wooster Pike and in the adjoining Linden Place cul-de-sac. Economy of materials and inexpensive construction guided the plans for this housing group and its community garage at the rear of the properties. The two architects had distinguished careers. Alfred Elzner studied with Frank Duveneck and was associated with H. H. Richardson of Boston when the Chamber of Commerce Building was constructed in Cincinnati. George Anderson joined him as partner in about 1896, and together they produced Cincinnati's famous Ingalls Building, considered the first reinforced concrete "skyscraper" in America.

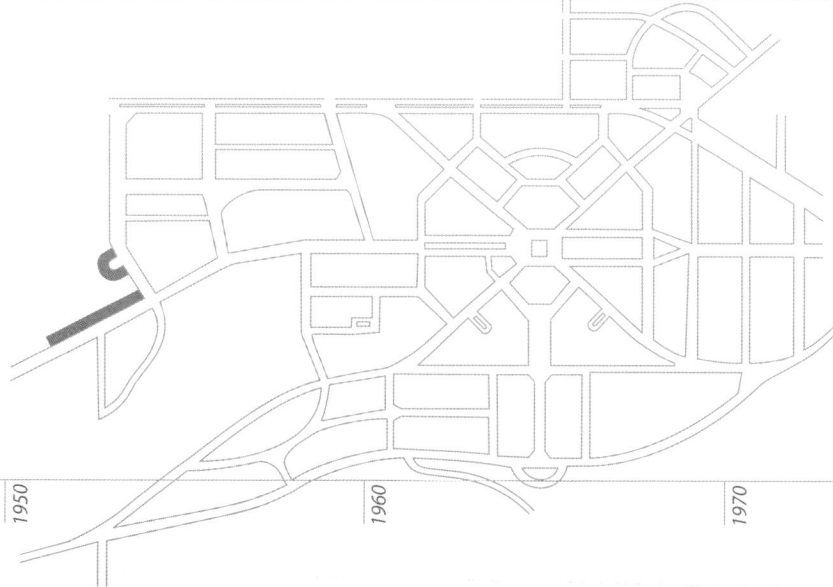

MARIEMONT
DEVELOPMENT · LINDEN PLACE
ELZNER & ANDERSON · ARCH'TS
1 9 · CINCINNATI · OHIO · 2 4

A promotional brochure for Mariemont was initiated by Charles J. Livingood to interest prospective renters and purchasers of building lots. The brochure's cover, designed by Russian American artist Andrew Avinoff, was required by Livingood to be "a picture as through a window of the Church, Cemetery, Dale Park, Dana houses, and a few houses on Cherry Lane with a lovely background of the hills behind"; "within we shall have the complete story of Mariemont, historical, as well as the possibilities of the Town." An early aerial photograph shows the old town square, town houses and apartment buildings, and nearly treeless streets and cemetery surrounding the church.

MARIEMONT·CINCINNATI·DISTRICT·OHIO·APARTMENTS·STORES AND GROUP HOUSING RIPLEY AND LE BOUTILLIER ARCHITECTS·BOSTON MA

In May 1924, work began on two apartment buildings at the corner of Oak and Chestnut Streets that anchored the town square in the Dale Park section and also provided conveniently located services and marketing for neighborhood residents. Boston architects Hubert Ripley and Addison LeBoutillier submerged the ground-floor shops into the mass of the mirror-image buildings. The apartment buildings are joined on Chestnut Street by a group of town houses by the same architects and designed in a modified Tudor Revival style.

Earliest Construction and Styles

One of the largest residential projects undertaken by the
Mariemont Company was the commission given to Philadelphia
architect Edmund B. Gilchrist. His string of thirty-nine town
houses was influenced by the eighteenth- and nineteenth-
century row houses he knew so well in his hometown. Gilchrist's
Georgian Revival–style units were built along the northern border
of Mariemont on Murray Avenue, with a few bending along
Plainville Road. Running across Maple Street at Plainville Road
is the so-called Honeymoon Apartment, a dramatic setting for a
small residence charmingly capped with a cupola. Livingood once
referred to it as a "perhaps foolish house over-the-street."

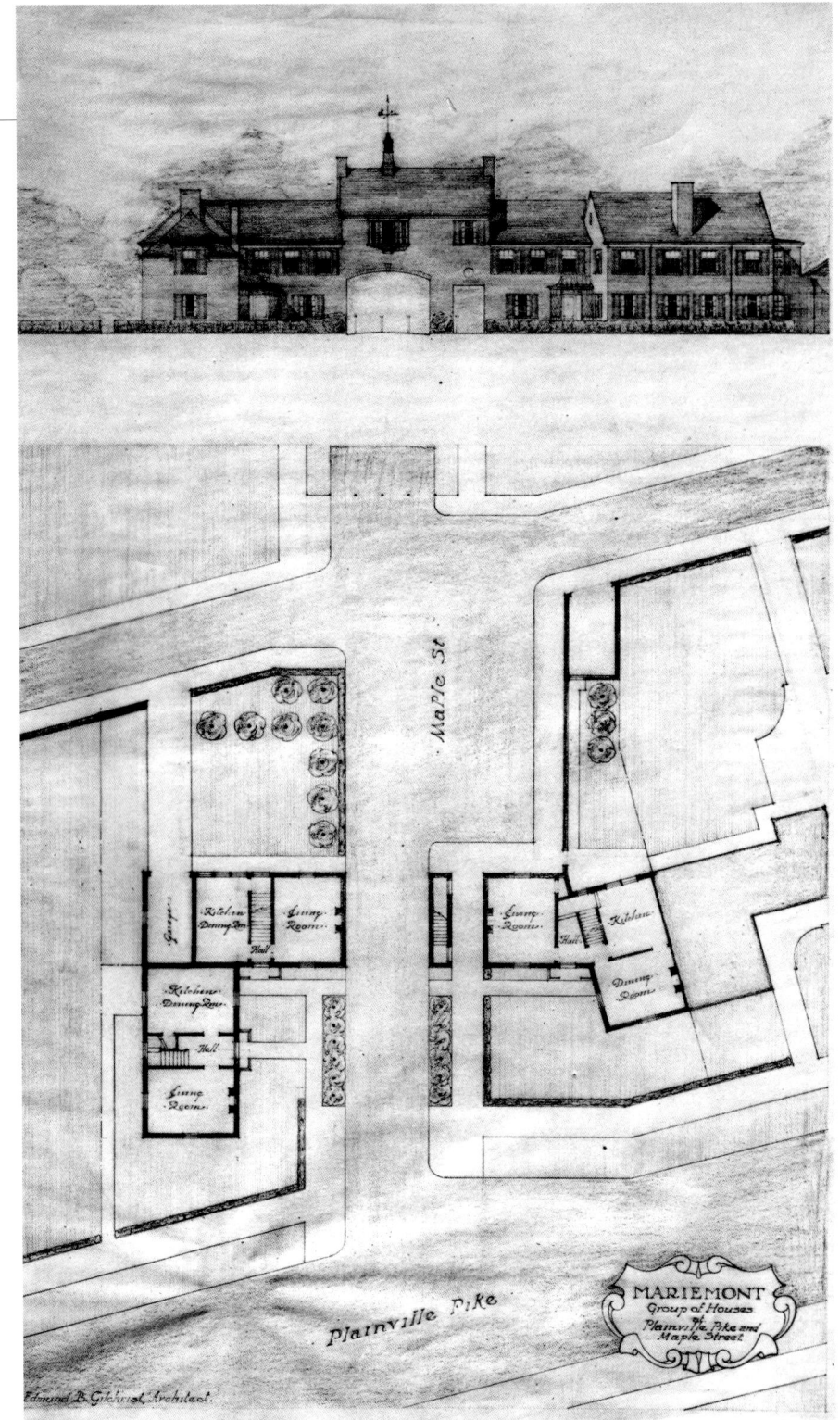

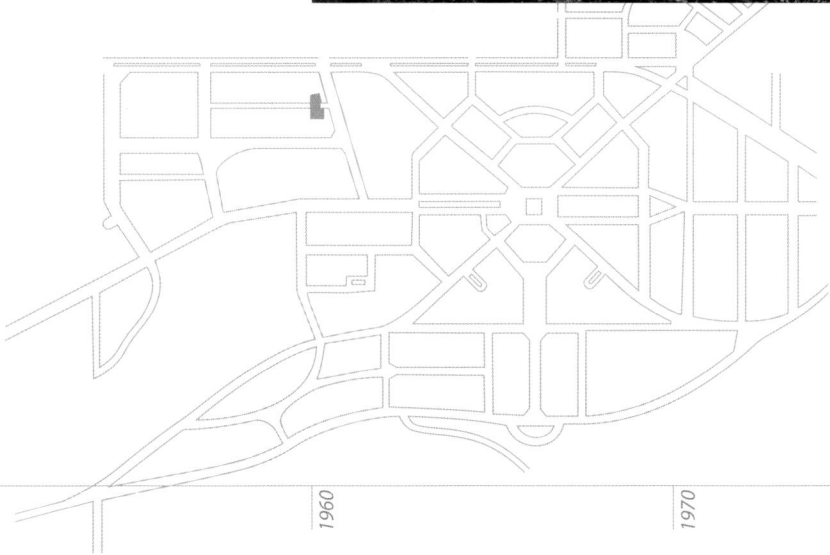

Earliest Construction and Styles

Early photograph of portion of Gilchrist Group, shutterless and before removal of overhead wires.

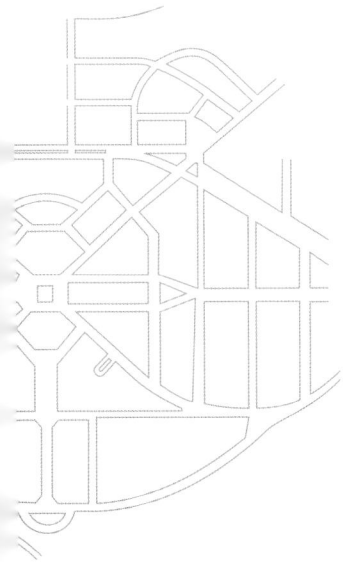

All of the architects commissioned by the Mariemont Company were accomplished at drawing elevations and settings for their buildings. Hubert Ripley was perhaps the most accomplished artist among them, but Edmund Gilchrist's delicately rendered peeks into pathways between his buildings show his talents.

Earliest Construction and Styles

Charles Cellarius was a prominent Cincinnati architect and an influential advisor on acceptable architectural styles and buildings who served long after the Mariemont Company dissolved in 1931. He designed residences, the Carillon structure, and the village's fire and police station. Built in 1924, the station is a kind of fanciful Hansel-and-Gretel cottage in Tudor Revival style, with timber-supported porch, small dormer, and peaked roof over the fire truck garage.

·CHAS·F·CELLARIUS·ARCHT·

Earliest Construction and Styles

It was Mary Emery's successful intention to establish Mariemont as an exemplar of American town planning with improved housing and amenities. In stark contrast to tenement living and overcrowded settlements, the village combined rental units in a suburban setting with single-family houses plus lots for purchasers to build for themselves. Richard H. Dana Jr., a New York architect, designed these first housing units for Mariemont.

1800   1900   1910   1920   1923   1930   1940

MARCH 6. 19

Development before Incorporation: 1925-1941

Mariemont's major years of construction following the Nolen plan effectively ended in 1925. By that date, the infrastructure was completed and Nolen's plan was beginning to become a reality, sprinkled with houses on the skeleton of streets. Livingood thought Nolen's services were no longer needed, and he was released at the end of 1925. Housing starts under the Mariemont Company ended in 1928, although some public buildings were still under construction. In 1929, the Recreation Building was the last structure to be built by the Mariemont Company, which dissolved in 1931. Its assets, including ownership of Mariemont, were turned over to the Thomas J. Emery Memorial, a charitable foundation formed by Mary Emery.

Mary Emery died in October 1927, and the Great Depression of 1929 wreaked havoc with the stock market, the nation's financial picture, and jobs. These events effectively ended the fulfillment of Mariemont, at least according to the Nolen plan and the original vision and direction, and were devastating blows to the continued progress of Mariemont's construction in the years leading to World War II.

In 1941, an attempt was made by the City of Cincinnati to annex Mariemont. Annexation was resisted by Mariemont residents, and incorporation followed that same year, creating the Village of Mariemont under Ohio law, with an elected government. The Emery Memorial did not object and turned its assets over to the newly formed village.

New York architect Louis E. Jallade was given the commission in 1923 for the Mariemont Community Church (originally called the Mariemont Memorial Church), to be built adjacent to the cemetery. Medieval in appearance and nondenominational in religion, the church, at Mary Emery's request, inaugurated the construction program for the rest of the town. The Norman-Gothic–style stone edifice recalled in its design and appearance numerous parish churches in England dating from the thirteenth and fourteenth centuries. Buttressed walls, steeply pitched roof, squat and square crossing tower, and pointed arch windows identify its architectural heritage.

Completion and Expansion to World War II

1922 Ford

Lots of bricks (labor)

10-21-24.

Dale Park School, designed in 1924 by Cincinnati architect Abraham Lincoln Fechheimer in a conservative Georgian Revival style and built by the Mariemont Company at a central location in the rental residential area, served the boys and girls of Mariemont as the community's elementary school from kindergarten through eighth grade.

The Ripley and LeBoutillier apartment buildings, right, that were an exact pair, formed a major focus at the intersection of Oak and Chestnut Streets. This view taken during the construction phase reflects building and transportation methods common in the early twentieth century. Construction at this site was concluded in 1925.

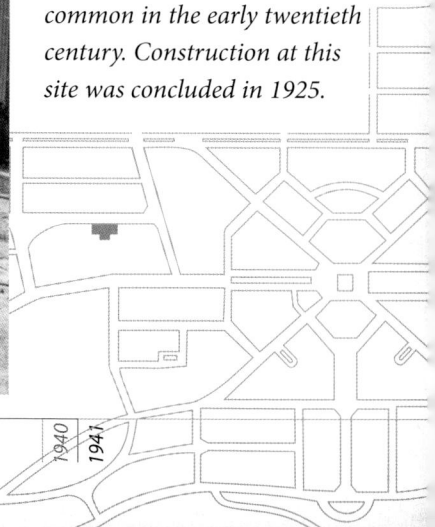

1800 1900 1910 1920 1925 1930 1940 1941

The large surveying crew for Mariemont was headed by Warren W. Parks, who was appointed resident engineer in 1923, just as groundbreaking occurred. He appears in the photograph in the front row, far left. His tenure lasted twenty years, from Mariemont's beginnings until its incorporation. Surveying projects of Mariemont's scale depended on extra surveyors supplied by students drawn from the Engineering Department of the University of Cincinnati. At right, footers are laid for the Mariemont Steam Plant, situated below the bluff, near the Little Miami River.

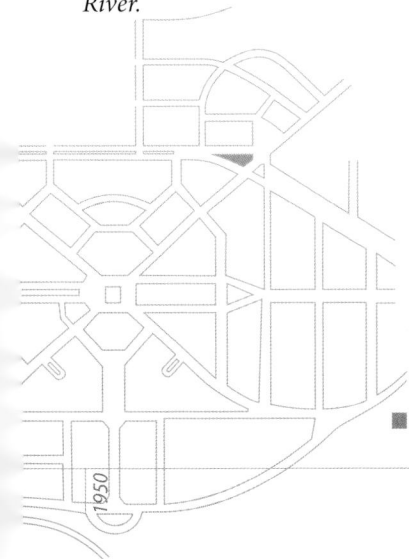

The last major building construction by the Mariemont Company was the Thomas J. Emery Recreation Hall, designed by New York architect George B. deGersdorff and erected in 1929–1930. Built to serve Mariemont residents with its gymnasium, bowling alleys, rifle range, and other amenities, it currently is the Parish Center of the Mariemont Community Church. The Italian Renaissance Revival style of the red brick building with clay tile roof echoes many churches and monasteries in Italy with its clock tower or campanile (bell tower), pillared arcade, and rounded walls resembling a church's apse.

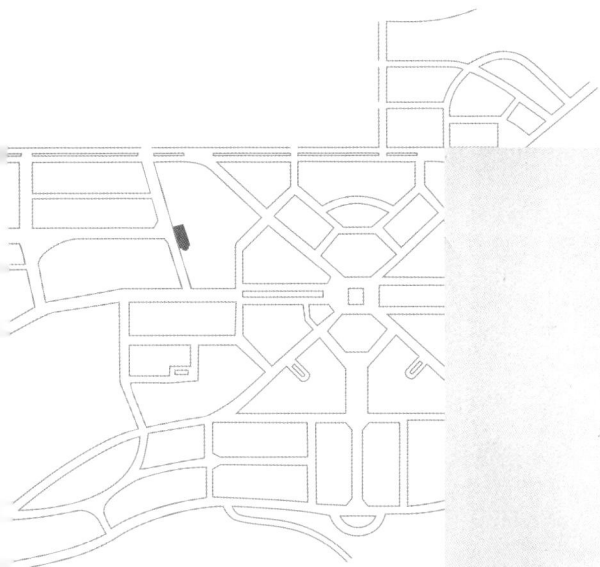

Mary Emery intended to build Resthaven Gardens, a section in
the northeast portion of Mariemont, as a complete retirement
neighborhood for workers in the Emery interests who had
"grown old in service and may have a comfortable home
amid pleasant surroundings for the remainder of their lives."
The design project by New York architect Hubert E. Reeves
included a colony of small houses, a barn, a working farm,
and a plant nursery, all in close proximity to the Mariemont
Hospital. Nolen's plan subdivided the area and assigned lots for
the various parts. Resthaven Barn was completed in 1924.

Early photographs commissioned by the Mariemont Company recorded buildings in their many phases of construction. By 1924, the new town was an anthill of activity, the busiest year in the building of Mariemont. Over a thousand workers in all trades worked on this labor-intensive project.

July 3, 1925

Construction of individual homes on the south side of Wooster Pike in 1924 focused on several niches where the Mariemont Company hoped to show examples of good architectural design and lure buyers of lots to build their own residences.

Perhaps the best-known landmark is the Mary M. Emery Carillon, a memorial gift from Isabella F. Hopkins, Mrs. Emery's sister, in 1929 and dedicated in 1930. The towering stone structure containing massive racks of bronze bells was designed by Cincinnati architect Charles F. Cellarius. Its frequent concerts in Dogwood Park are an attractive background for the good life in Mariemont.

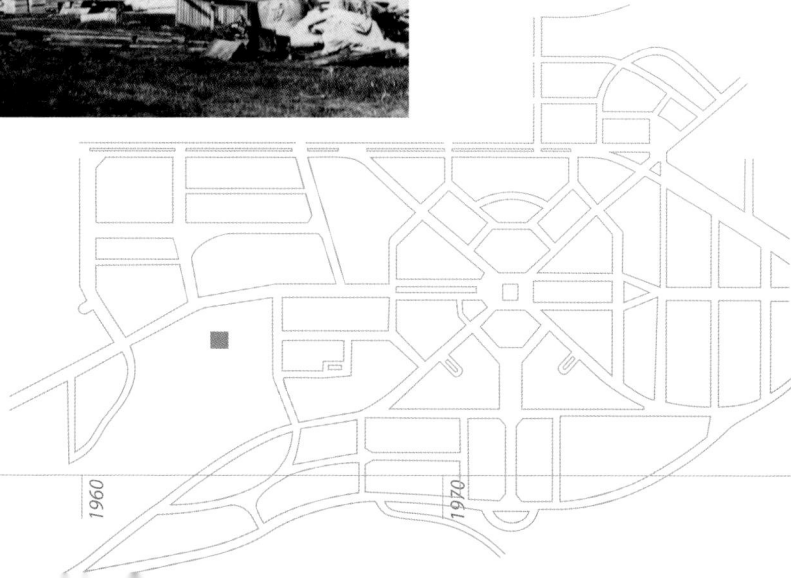

9-19-29

Photographs taken during construction usually illustrate some of the building processes and techniques required to translate plans to realized structures. The examples of Sheldon Close (left) and the Ziegler Group on Chestnut Street (right), taken during construction in 1924–25, also show the obvious talents of architects Grosvenor Atterbury and Carl A. Ziegler, respectively, in maintaining the persistent Tudor Revival architectural style established for Mariemont.

10-28-24.

The Mariemont Company, under Charles J. Livingood's direction, intended the town square in the village's heart to be the center of "the throbbing, busy life of the community." It was to be filled with fifty shops, a theater, and an inn, all clustered in Tudor Revival style and half-timbered elegance.

A Cincinnati firm, Joseph Steinkamp and Brother, was commissioned to design the arcade building. Drawings were produced by Steinkamp, but the expansive building was never realized. Only the Mariemont Inn was built. The site remained undeveloped until 1938, when a theater building and its adjoining shops were built on the entire north frontage of the town square.

MARIEMONT PHARMACY
RENTED

HOME OF THE MARIEMONT MOVIE

10-12-38

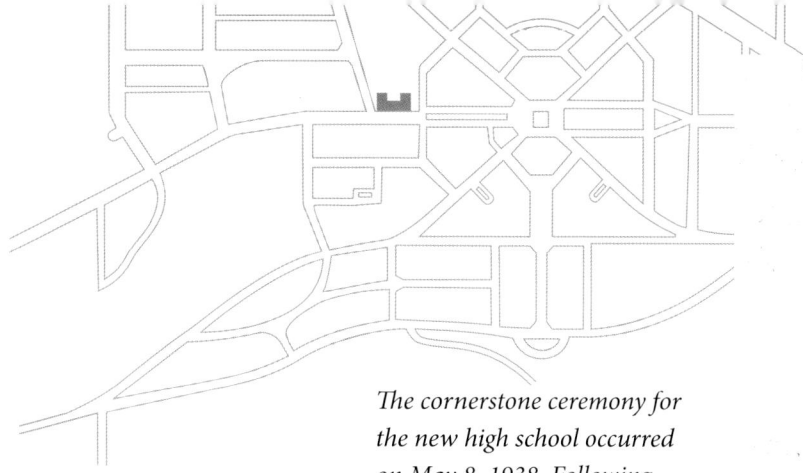

At a prominent location on Wooster Pike at Plainville Road, a spot John Nolen designated in his 1921 plan, excavation began in 1937 for the Plainville School District's high school building. A frame house at the corner was saved and moved to a new location on Pocahontas Avenue. Mariemont's first school was this long frame building located originally on Wooster Pike. It served Mariemont's children until Dale Park School was completed.

The cornerstone ceremony for the new high school occurred on May 8, 1938. Following incorporation of Mariemont in 1941, the Mariemont School District was formed, and the name of the new high school was changed.

Emerging from the site at the well-attended cornerstone ceremony in the spring of 1938, the new high school building, designed by Cincinnati architect E. C. Landberg, is an impressive example of Georgian Revival architecture. Interestingly, the façade resembles one of the visionary drawings by Hubert Ripley done in 1922 for a town hall that was rejected. The building serves today as the Mariemont Elementary School.

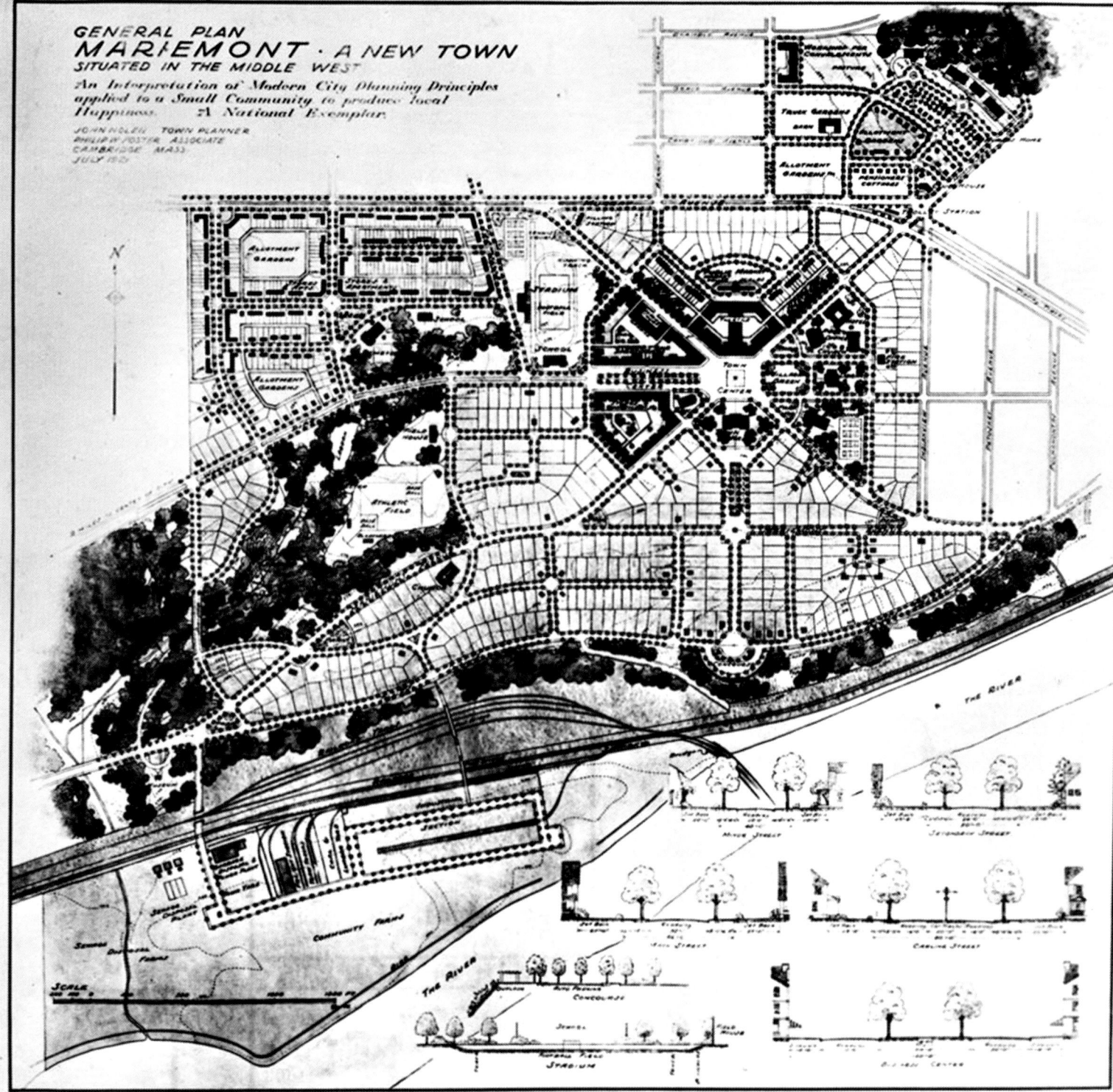

GENERAL PLAN
MARIEMONT · A NEW TOWN
SITUATED IN THE MIDDLE WEST

An Interpretation of Modern City Planning Principles
applied to a Small Community to produce local
Happiness.   A National Exemplar.

JOHN NOLEN TOWN PLANNER
PHILIP W. FOSTER ASSOCIATE
CAMBRIDGE MASS.
JULY 1921

The axial street pattern of Mariemont's center, along with curving roadways, wooded areas, and the many undeveloped lots, shows clearly in aerial photographs made during the construction period in the 1920s. Rental housing appears near the top edge of the aerial photograph. The Little Miami River appears at the lower left corner of the photograph and forms the southern border of the new town.

Completion and Expansion to World War II

Photographs taken from low-flying airplanes were not common in the 1920s. These rare views of Mariemont from 1926 and 1929 show completed construction of Mariemont Company buildings as well as a few individual residences scattered over the landscape. When Livingood acquired the Indianview section, adjacent to the town square's eastern edge, in 1922, he complained to Nolen that he was acquiring property "rather wildly." At right, the new acquisition appears in three parallel streets, Indianview, Petoskey, and Pocahontas, at the lower edge of the photograph. It added fifty-five acres to Mary Emery's holdings.

1950 1960 1970 1980 1990 2000

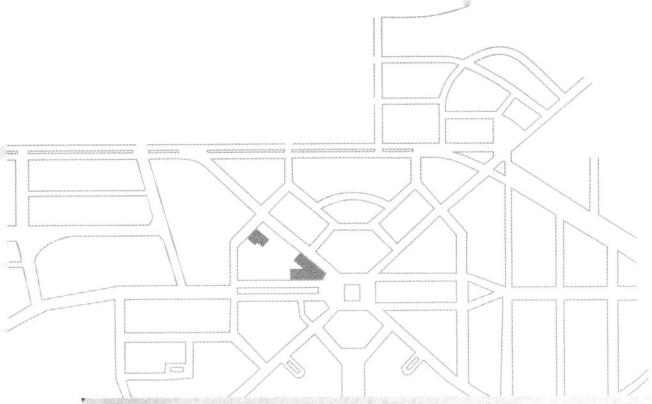

The Mariemont Inn opened for business in April 1929, after serving as office space for its owner, the Mariemont Company, from 1925. In the Inn building, which was smaller than the architects designed, there were a few shops on the ground floor, a tearoom, a restaurant, and a solarium. The Inn operated a garage on its grounds for car repairs and service. That site is now occupied by the Executive Building. Immediately to the rear of the Inn was an open-air terrace for dining, called the Summer Garden, where dances, movies, and social events in the summer season were popular. The Mariemont Company sold the Inn to private ownership in 1945.

Originally, Dale Park School had a spacious and windowed kindergarten at the rear that overlooked a creek and grassy field. As the elementary school population grew, additions eliminated the rear façade.

The entire Dale Park School faculty and student body, filling ten classrooms from kindergarten through eighth grade, spread along Chestnut Street for their photograph in 1925–26.

The streetcar line along a green space north of Murray Avenue served early residents long before Mariemont was founded. Originally called the Cincinnati, Milford, and Blanchester line, it was a private enterprise and was later operated by the Mariemont Company. By 1927, the line was operated by Cincinnati Street Railway system. Route 71 became known as the Mariemont Line. The last streetcar run to and from Mariemont occurred on January 6, 1942.

Livingood wrote to Nolen early in 1921 about his interest in an "ambitious central heating plant not only for the Institutional Tract but for the central properties and as much surrounding them as can be safely undertaken."

By 1925, the heating plant was functioning, creating steam heat for many residences and businesses through a complex underground tunnel system. Nearly three-fourths of the residences were served by this heating system, but it was abandoned in 1954, by which time heating was provided by furnaces in individual homes.

Near Merrimont
WORLD'S "MODEL" CITY
FOR SALE
2 LOTS
INQUIRE
6225 MADISON RD.   Phone MAD. 65

Sign on Plainville Pike.

Just north of Mariemont line

Selling the New Town: 1925-1930

Marketing a Way of Life

As noted in *John Nolen and Mariemont: Building a New Town in Ohio,* "After Mary Emery's death in 1927, Mariemont retreated from its energetic beginnings and its frenzied construction. There was a sense of prosperity and fulfillment in the village, however, as new residents moved into their rented apartments and houses." But as early as 1922, before the official groundbreaking, the Mariemont Company sought buyers who might build on lots they purchased, advertising with large wooden signs placed prominently around Mariemont and in newspapers. Bold headlines touted "a self-contained village to house in ideal surroundings ten thousand people"—"Stop at the quaint English inn and visit its model homes . . ."—"All wires underground."

Marketing efforts sometimes made spelling errors, as in this large sign marking lots available for purchase in the open space in the new development of "Merrimont."

The Mariemont Preservation Foundation houses a large archive devoted to the village's history. In the collection are many yellowed pages from the advertisements placed in the 1920s by the Mariemont Company to lure renters and purchasers of lots to the new town.

THURSDAY, SEPTEMBER 3, 1925— **THE D**

HOUSES FOR RENT. HOUSES FOR RENT

Spend Labor Day at

MARIEMONT
"THE NEW TOWN"
A National Exemplar

Labor Day Festival

Come out to Mariemont on Labor Day and be the guests of the beautiful "new town" that everybody is talking about. Come out and be cool and happy in the shade of the forest trees. Make free use of the Auto Camp, with city water and cooking facilities. Plenty of parking room for all the autos in Cincinnati.

Programmes Afternoon and Evening

You can go all around Mariemont, personally conducted by our guides, and see the many points of interest. But don't forget the special events of the afternoon and evening.

Be sure to visit Mariemont on Labor Day. Bring your family, your friends and yourself.

AFTERNOON SPORTS

Full programme of outdoor sports, Track and Field Events where you can witness them in the cool shade of the high forest trees that surround the great field. Ball game on the town's ball grounds.

CONCERT IN EVENING

Spend the evening on the cool, breezy concourse that looks down on the wide Miami Valley. Programme of popular music by Cincinnati's best—the famous Weber's Band of 40 pieces—from 7:30 to 9:30 p. m.

MOVING PICTURES WILL BE TAKEN OF THE AFTERNOON EVENTS. COME WITHIN RANGE OF THE CAMERA AND LATER SEE YOURSELF ON THE SCREEN AT KEITH'S.

THE MARIEMONT COMPANY

May 16, 1930

COME TO MARIEMONT TODAY!

Ramble in the woods---
Visit the school and church---
Enjoy a real dinner at the Inn—
Play Golf or Tennis—
Spend a day in the Open—
Hear the Carillon at 3:30 p. m.—
Buy or rent a Home—
Rent a House or Apartment—
Choose a Lot for your very own.

HOW TO COME!

Use Your Sunday Pass on This City Street Car

Fifth and Main
Gilbert Ave.
Peebles Cor.
Madison Road
or
Erie Avenue
Direct Service

Ride the Mariemont Line, Fountain Square to Mariemont

Cincinnati Street Railway Motor Coach Route A. The Big 6-Wheelers. Government Square To the Mariemont Inn via Madison Road Every 15 Minutes.

The City Transit Green Mariemont Bus. Government Square To Mariemont via Observatory Road, Linwood Road and Eastern Avenue Every Few Minutes.

Or Drive Out Erie Avenue or Eastern Avenue

General Plan MARIEMONT A New Town

Cincinnati District,   *"A National Exemplar"*   Ohio, U. S.

The Village of Mariemont comprising 420 Acres, largely high-lying, slightly rolling, naturally-drained farmland overlooking the Little Miami Valley, lies nine miles east from Cincinnati's business center, just outside the corporation limits.

The main lines of the Pennsylvania R.R. and of the Norfolk & Western R.R. intersect on the property, while the Baltimore & Ohio R.R. and the Chicago Division of the Pennsylvania pass nearby. A State Highway from the capital city, Columbus, to Cincinnati runs east and west through the Town Center, and broad diagonal roads and the Boulevard lead to the hill-top suburbs and at grade to the heart of the metropolis.

The site was selected for its nearness to the city, in a clean, healthy locality, easy of access, with Norwood, Ohio and the "factory colonies" of Oakley and Hyde Park only two miles distant to the west.

Mariemont has a completed sewer system, city water, natural gas, and Cincinnati telephone and electric light by underground conduits, to every lot in the village.

A central Heating Plant with mains serving three-fourths of the property.

Nine miles of modern streets, paved and planted.

50 acres of parks, playgrounds, village greens and floral gardens.

On the Boulevard, two miles long, are recreation fields and a large shaded Concourse for public gatherings, with extensive views of the Little Miami River from Milford on the east to its junction with the Ohio River at the foot of the Kentucky hills opposite Cincinnati.

Mariemont is primarily a residential district intended for wage earners of different economic grades.

Its houses and buildings will be of stone, brick, stucco, and frame contruction, single homes predominating.

For details regarding plan of development of Mariemont, advantages, restrictions, etc., see within.

An Interpretation of Modern City Planning Principles applied to a small Self-Contained Community to produce Local Happiness.

John Nolen, *Town Planner*
Philip W. Foster, *Associate*
Cambridge, Mass.

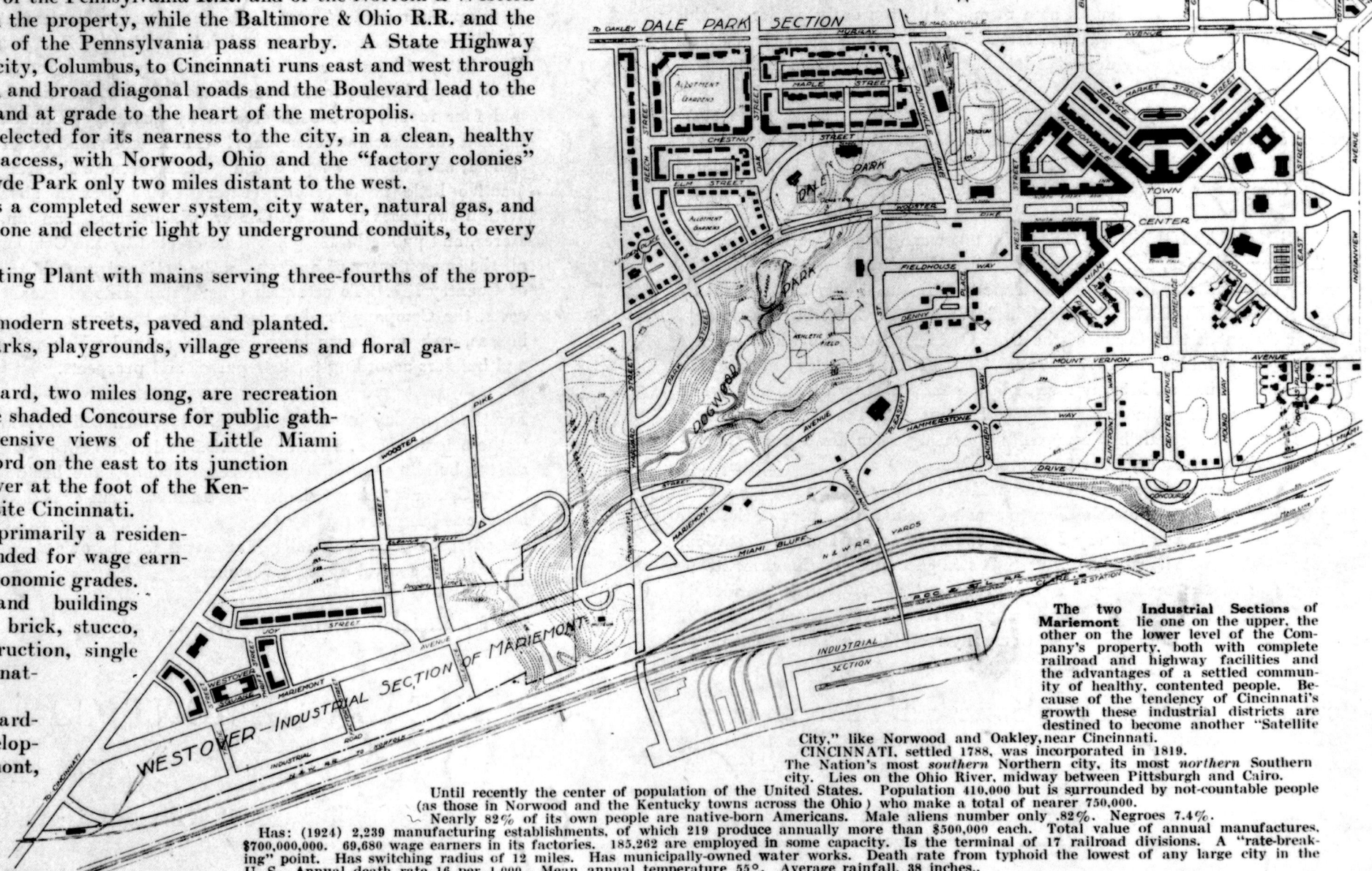

The two Industrial Sections of Mariemont lie one on the upper, the other on the lower level of the Company's property, both with complete railroad and highway facilities and the advantages of a settled community of healthy, contented people. Because of the tendency of Cincinnati's growth these industrial districts are destined to become another "Satellite City," like Norwood and Oakley, near Cincinnati.

CINCINNATI, settled 1788, was incorporated in 1819.

The Nation's most *southern* Northern city, its most *northern* Southern city. Lies on the Ohio River, midway between Pittsburgh and Cairo.

Until recently the center of population of the United States. Population 410,000 but is surrounded by not-countable people (as those in Norwood and the Kentucky towns across the Ohio) who make a total of nearer 750,000.

Nearly 82% of its own people are native-born Americans. Male aliens number only .82%. Negroes 7.4%.

Has: (1924) 2,239 manufacturing establishments, of which 219 produce annually more than $500,000 each. Total value of annual manufactures, $700,000,000. 69,680 wage earners in its factories. 185,262 are employed in some capacity. Is the terminal of 17 railroad divisions. A "rate-breaking" point. Has switching radius of 12 miles. Has municipally-owned water works. Death rate from typhoid the lowest of any large city in the U. S. Annual death rate 16 per 1,000. Mean annual temperature 55°. Average rainfall, 38 inches..

For further information address

THE MARIEMONT COMPANY
Chas. J. Livingood, *Prest.*   Thomas Hogan, Jr., *Secty.*
No. 1 Baker Court, Cincinnati, Ohio

1800   1900   1910   1920   1925   1930   1940

Nolen's 1921 plan was enlarged with additional land purchases by Mrs. Emery, notably the Indianview section and an industrial area called Westover. By 1925 the published plan was amended to include these additions, and the plan then recorded its size as 420 acres.

Like Magic!
CENTRAL HEAT
CLEAN
STEADY
DEPENDABLE

Why Worry About the Cold Weather?

Mariemont has 250 acres of homes heated from a single Central Heating Plant. Giant well-insulated lines carry steam underground direct from the plant on the Pennsylvania R. R., into each house. In Mariemont we give no more concern to our heat than we do to our electric, gas or water supply. See our window display at 115 East Fourth St.

No Furnaces   On Day and Night
No Coal   Silent
No Ashes   Automatic
No Soot   Low Cost

Turn it on or off as water at your sink.

MARIEMONT
The New Town

Central Heated Houses For Rent
6 or 7 Rooms $68.75 to $90.
Garages, Heat, Water Included.

Central Heated Apartments
3-4-5 Rooms—$30 to $40.
Hot and Cold Water, Heat, Janitor, Kitchens equipped.

Dale Park Houses Individual Furnaces
5 or 6 Rooms, Water Included. $30-$50.

Take Mariemont Street Car or Bus,
Drive out Erie Ave. or Eastern Ave.

ASK MR. FAGLEY,
AT THE MARIEMONT INN.
TEL. BRamble 1300.
Downtown Office, 110 E. 4th St.
TEL. MAin 1231.

THE THOMAS J. EMERY MEMORIAL

Advertisements issued by the Mariemont Company promoted amenities that prospective buyers and renters sought. "Like Magic! Central Heat—Clean—Steady—Dependable—Why worry about the cold weather?" recommended the steam-heating system available in Mariemont.

Houses For Rent.   Houses For Rent.   Houses For Rent.

MARIEMONT
THE NEW TOWN

IT'S RIGHT ALONGSIDE CINCINNATI, not "way out in the wilds," as some suppose. KNOW for yourself. Look at the map. ITS TOWN CENTER is nearer Fountain Square than the heart of Madisonville.

IT has broad, well-paved streets, lighted by electricity; sidewalks, sewers, city water, gas, electric, telephone service at city rates, a fire department even, and house-to-house postal delivery.

IT has shops: Kroger, Fenton, Model Laundry, Drug, Delicatessen, Barber, Dry Goods, The Fourth-Central Bank.

IT has a fine grade school, church, community club and everything needed to make home life enjoyable.

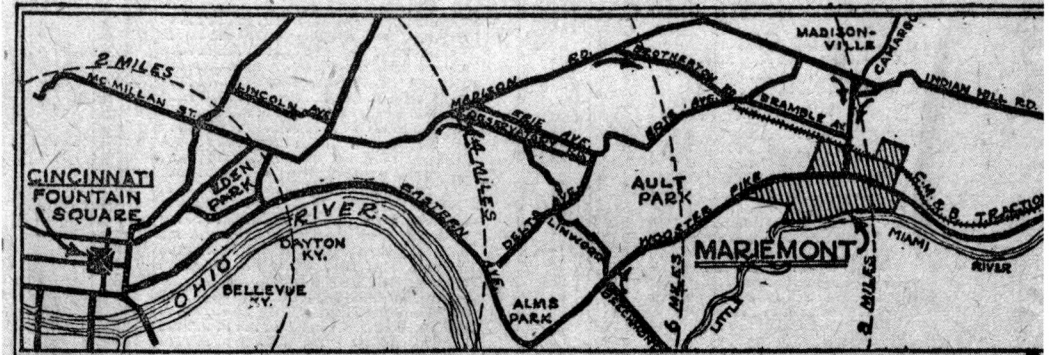

BUY OR RENT A HOME NOW
Come Out Today

Houses—4, 5, 6 Rooms, $35, $45, $55, $60.
Apartments—1, 2, 3, 4, 5 Rooms, $25, $30, $40, $60, $65, $70.

HOUSES STEAM HEATED 24 HOURS A DAY FROM CENTRAL PLANT, $90, $100.

Drive out the road nearest you or take Madisonville car to Kroger Line.

Direct Bus Service From Fountain Square.

THE MARIEMONT CO.

Madisonville 1300.   City Office—No. 1 Baker Court.   Main 2395.

See Inside Cover of Your Telephone Directory.

Bringing Mary Emery's Dream to Life

Mary Emery's love for children was evidenced in many ways. Among the many philanthropies that she founded or financed with her husband was the Hospital of the Protestant Episcopal Church (1884); a new, larger building in Mount Auburn (1887) that later evolved into Cincinnati's Children's Hospital; and the Babies Milk Fund (1909). Perhaps the loss of her two sons encouraged this devotion to improving the lives of children. The three children of Charles J. Livingood became especially close to her, spending many summer months living nearby in Mariemont, Rhode Island. In this photograph, Mary Emery stands with Elizabeth Livingood, the youngest child, ca. 1912.

On October 1, 1924, a town house on Chestnut Street welcomed the first family to move into a home in the rental section.

In November 1935, Hamilton County Deputy Sheriff Chris Robisch was employed by the Thomas J. Emery Memorial to head the village's police department. Beginning with the title of marshal, he became chief of police by the newly elected council after incorporation. Chief Robisch was a long-serving, much beloved figure in the village.

Police protection for Mariemont, like the elementary school and fire department, was originally under the control of and financed by the Mariemont Company.

Among Chief Robisch's pleasant duties was his work with and encouragement of the safety patrol boys and girls for Dale Park School.

The first elected officials for the
newly incorporated village were
sworn into office on June 27,
1941: E. Boyd Jordan, Mayor
(center, back row), and Clerk
W. F. Keown, Treasurer E. L.
MacArthur, Town Marshal
Chris Robisch, and Council
Members Julian Bailey, Byron
Board, Gordon Jones, Ann
Buntin-Becker, Russell Geil,
and Harry Mohlman.

E. Boyd Jordan served as Mariemont's first mayor, beginning in
1941 after incorporation and continuing for eight consecutive
terms until his death in 1959. He was also the choir director for
the Mariemont Community Church and the village's carillonneur.

1800   1900   1910   1920   1925   1930   1940 1941

An event of national
importance occurred in 1931
when the Junior League of
America held its annual
meeting in the Mariemont
Recreation Hall (later
the Parish Center of the
Mariemont Community
Church). The building's
façade, bell tower, and
arcade present an impressive
and unique example of
Italianate architectural style
in Mariemont. The building
was completed in 1930, the
last major construction project
undertaken by the Mariemont
Company.

The Outdoors: 1921-1960

John Nolen was an experienced landscape architect before he became more active as a town planner, and his expertise in the former profession was always evidenced in his work with hundreds of communities he planned during his career. Nolen's task with Mariemont was to prepare a plan in which people's needs integrated, not subjugated, the landscape, to create pleasant neighborhoods, and to promote an accessible community. When his plan was superimposed on the farmland, woods, and creeks, he sought harmony and harmonious marriage of site and plan. The natural beauty of the landscape always dominated Nolen's perceptions.

Nolen's 1921 plan covered 253 acres. Over fifty acres were devoted to parks, with about eighty acres remaining at the scenic southern edge of the village and within the floodplain of the Little Miami River. Some parks were intended to be manicured and used for baseball and soccer fields; others were left densely wooded. Pocket parks and scenic vistas were placed throughout the village. Outstanding examples of Nolen's approach in emphasizing and preserving the natural landscape are displayed in the grassy median strip centering the main thoroughfare in Mariemont, the beech woods at the town square, the impressive overlook and Concourse above the Little Miami River, Dale Park, and Dogwood Park and its twelve acres of woods and creek.

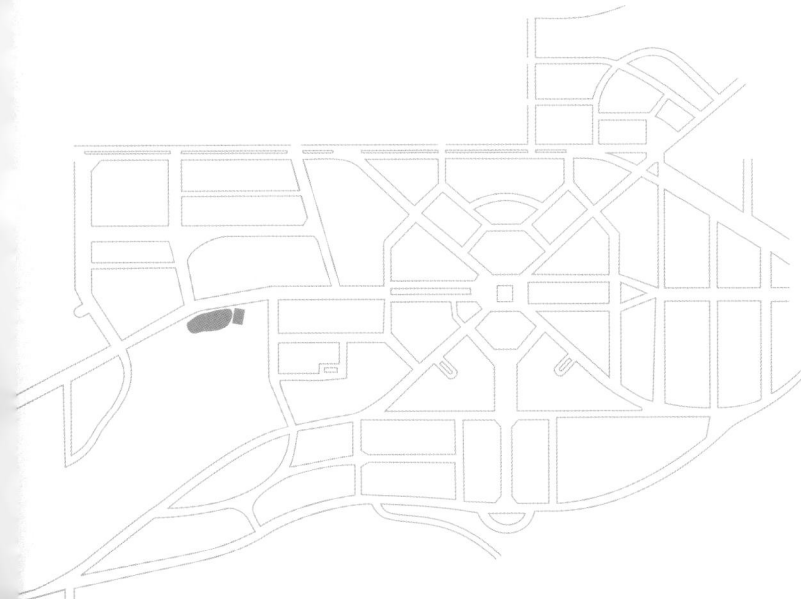

The picturesque swan gliding on the small lake in front of the Boat House was a favorite subject of photographers visiting this Mariemont setting.

Landscape and Activities

1800   1900   1910   1920 1921   1930   1940

Mariemont parks provided baseball and soccer fields, as well as
locations for unusual events, such as the "baby and doll parade"
recorded in this photograph from the 1920s.

Dale Park was designed by Nolen with playfields, sloping lawns bordering a narrow creek, and flower gardens. Taking a cue from the beautiful gardens in the English planned communities that enthralled Livingood, he planned a small portion to provide well-manicured flower beds at a busy traffic corner, Wooster Pike at Plainville Road. At this location, the Mariemont Company placed The Family Group, a sculpture by the French artist Lucien Alliot, probably dating from the early 1920s. It exemplifies Mary Emery's love of children in its depiction of three generations of a family: children, parents, and grandparents. It has long served as symbol of Mariemont's welcoming nature and its many amenities that make the town so attractive to families.

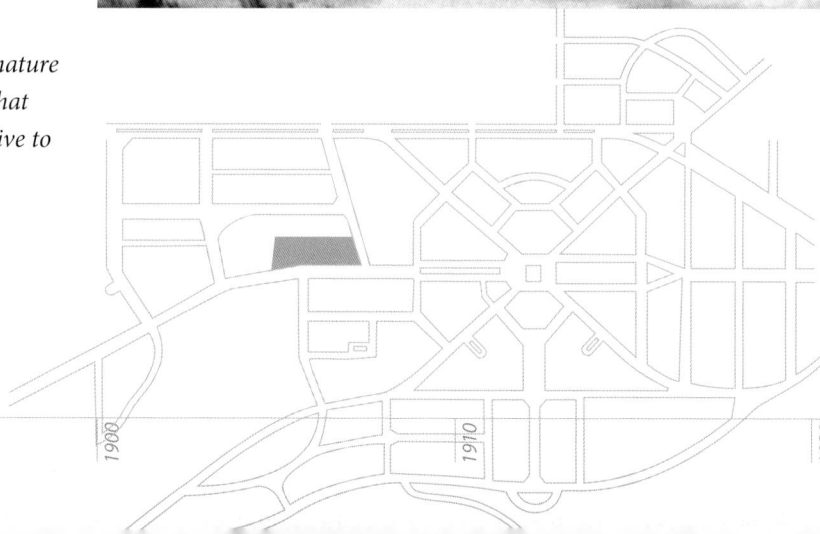

Nolen's reverence for the Mariemont site and its topography parallels the establishment of many national and state parks during the first decades of the twentieth century. He insisted on the need for parks and recreational areas as basic components of any town plan. The undulating sweep of this area separates the busy traffic on Wooster Pike from the many town houses and Dale Park School, providing a quiet divide in the Dale Park section.

1800   1900   1910   1920   1921   1930   1940

Landscape and Activities

The Boat House in Dogwood Park, a fanciful building with sharply peaked roof and thick stone walls built into an embankment, was designed by Cincinnati architect Charles Cellarius in 1927–28. The flat stones covering the roof mimic the medieval roof stones on the Mariemont Community Church. From any angle, the lagoon and Boat House formed a magical duet graced by swans, benches for relaxing, and a background of trees and shrubs. John Nolen's 1921 plan refers to a "Bath House" on a different site in Dogwood Park, apparently with the thought that it might be a facility for swimming. His proposal was never realized.

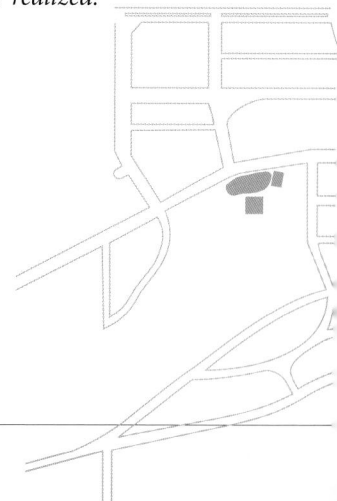

1800   1900   1910   1920 1921   1930   1940

Bordering a small lagoon intended for canoeing in summer and ice skating in winter, the Boat House, in its wooded setting, provided much enjoyment for the many Mariemont youngsters who paddled their fleets on sunny days. About 1945 the two-acre shallow lake was filled in, and the lagoon area became a pasture adjoining Whiskey Creek, which winds behind the Carillon and empties into the Little Miami River.

Landscape and Activities

The Concourse, a graceful arc of wood and stone, drips with wisteria vines and commands a dramatic view high above the Little Miami River. Designed by Nolen's associate designer, Philip W. Foster, and constructed in 1924, it terminates the long axis of Center Street and forms a magnificent allée of trees bordered by Tudor Revival–style homes. Livingood called the Concourse "the center of the greatest gatherings and towards evening will be a delightful spot for the inhabitants to congregate, for it has this great advantage—the sun does not set in the eyes of the visitor."

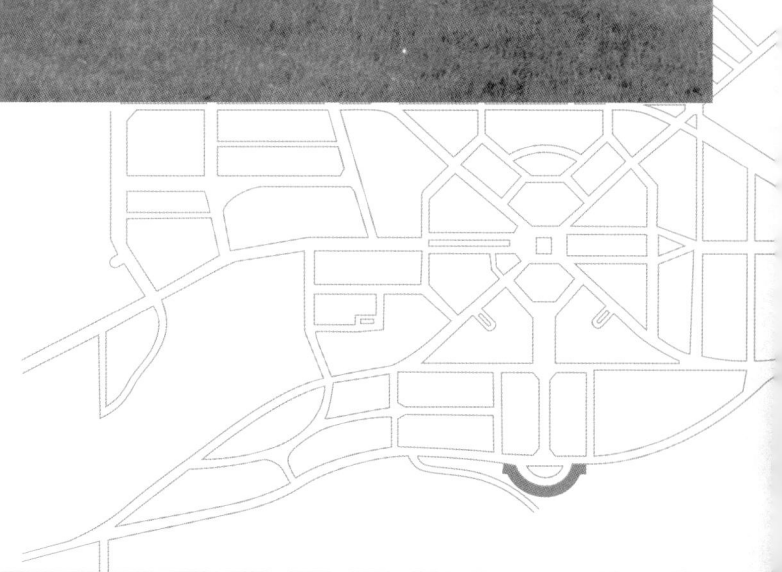

1800   1900   1910   1920 1921   1930   1940

An Artist Interprets Mariemont's Beauty: 1926

Nancy Ford Cones, Photographer

In 1906, an unknown photographer, Nancy Ford Cones, living on a farm outside of Loveland, Ohio, entered a competition sponsored by Eastman Kodak Company, then the world's greatest manufacturer of cameras and film. She placed second among twenty-eight thousand entries, ahead of the well-known artist and photographer Alfred Stieglitz and behind only the eminent Edward Steichen. Her work embraced the simple scenes she found near her farm home and in country byways. Sharing her artistry with her husband, James Cones, who developed all of her negatives until his death in 1939, she also received commissions for portraits and from popular magazines and corporations, such as Eastman Kodak and Bausch and Lomb. In 1926, the Mariemont Company provided Nancy, her husband, and daughter with a rent-free home on Oak and Elm Streets to employ her sensitive eye in photographing the beauties of Mariemont's buildings, woods, and activities. The Mariemont Preservation Foundation collection includes twenty-five photographs of Mariemont by Nancy Ford Cones that resulted from this yearlong stay.

During her one-year residency in Mariemont with her family in 1926, Nancy Ford Cones captured the beauty of the new town's architecture, showing the structures, such as the Concourse, almost as stage settings filled with the drama of light and shadow she saw in her camera's lens.

With her husband and daughter, Cones lived at 3875 Oak Street in one of the houses designed by Cincinnati architect Charles W. Short. Her black-and-white photographs during this period in her career were soft-focus, somewhat fuzzy, showing her allegiance to the aesthetic of the group of photographers who fostered Pictorialism in the early twentieth century.

The solitude and tranquil scene in woods on both sides of westbound Wooster Pike offers a peek in the distance of the Mariemont Inn.

1800   1900   1910   1920   1926   1930   1940

Children frequently modeled for Cones's photographs, as in this image of young neighbor Dorothy Booth conversing through an open window framed by hollyhocks. The photographer's daughter, Margaret, often posed for her mother, sometimes in costume, occasionally in a casual domestic moment. A few times Cones captured children at play, such as this summer scene under the sprinkler.

1800   1900   1910   1920   **1926**   1930   1940

Mariemont after World War II: 1941-1960

As the Great Depression waned in the late 1930s, the economy started to recover, but then World War II began, destroying lives and property on an unimaginable scale. The United States entered the conflict in 1941. Construction workers and building materials were drained away by war and defense needs, and many residential projects and projected public buildings in Mariemont were never realized.

Rentals of town houses and apartments slowed between 1931 and 1941. Many remained vacant. Only a small number of building lots were sold in this decade. Fewer individual homes were built, but a few rental apartment buildings were completed due to federal government encouragement via its FHA program. A popular apartment example in the 1950s and 1960s was the four-unit building, developed to satisfy renters and returning veterans. Shortly after the end of the war in 1945, residential construction started vigorously. In the 1950s, home building followed two paths in Mariemont. First was the production of custom homes, mostly rather small, on choice lots and designed by local architects. Second was the growing role of real estate developers, who purchased large numbers of lots, put up model homes, and then sold examples to buyers.

Buildings produced by the Mariemont Company in the 1920s are better examples of pure revival design and style, with quality craftsmanship and better recollection of historical elements than in those structures erected in the 1940s and later. Revival styles continued to be favored into the 1960s and beyond in both commercial and residential buildings.

There were losses by the 1950s of some of Mariemont's unique features. The elaborate underground steam-heating system for many homes was shut down because of maintenance costs and homeowners wanting better heating equipment. The lagoon at the Boat House, enjoyed for canoeing in summer and ice-skating in winter, was filled in when it became too costly to clean. And the Recreation Center, a magnificent Romanesque Revival multistory building with mock campanile that housed a gymnasium, bowling alley, rifle range, and meeting rooms, was sold by the village to the Mariemont Community Church.

The rush to complete much-needed housing in the first years after World War II was experienced in Mariemont. Four-family apartment buildings, often in Tudor Revival style, such as this example built in 1950, were not as excellently crafted as structures in a similar style from the 1920s. However, the later buildings echoed the persistent style in their shallow, half-timbered look with small bits of stuccowork.

In 1962, Mariemont's fire and police departments, along with offices for village administration, were housed in a Georgian Revival brick building with a view over the town square. The site originally housed the "hut" for the local American Legion post.

From the original plan for the town square, the centerpiece for the new town, only the massive Inn was completed by the Mariemont Company. The elaborate three-story building with its shops, arcade, and offices on the square's north side never was built. Fronting the south side of the town square, an office building built in 1957 faintly suggests the Tudor Revival style in its pediment over the main entrance. This structure and a rank of smaller buildings on the same side of the square expanded commercial development in the decade after World War II.

1950   1960   1970   1980   1990   2000

Growth in the Post-War Years

6961 Murray Ave. Mariemont   Job 122   1949

In the first few years after the end of World War II, developers quickly provided apartment housing in Mariemont, adopting primarily conservative architectural design compatible with the town's history. Few names of architects involved in the design, if any, are known, as most developers employed in-house architects and the plans carry only the company name. Among the Cincinnati developers and builders in this busy construction period are Myers Y. Cooper Company, McClure Company, Sibcy Company, and Dugan and Myers Company.

SIX ULTRA-
MODERN HOMES

LOCATED
MT. VERNON AND
FLINTPOINT WAY

UNDER
CONSTRUCTION
FOR THE
MARKET

Mariemont IS NOW IN KING'S ROW

ALLTIME SALES RECORD . . .

Sales of lots valued at $450,000.00 were made in the Town of Mariemont in the year 1946 which was a record unequalled in the sale of residential lots in the Cincinnati area. This gives a graphic picture of what is ahead for Mariemont's future growth and development.

Mariemont has moved into King's Row in new housing projects due to land sales during the past year.

There is a reason! The town was designed for gracious living, clean and healthful environment, suitable restrictions as to character of business and construction of homes.

Nor is that all. A home in Mariemont means less drudgery due to a Centralized heating system which insures cleanliness—a real joy to the housewife. Here is the great advantage: no furnaces to fire—turn on or off the heat at will, and best of all you make a substantial saving by the elimination of your heating system.

The comprehensive scheme of planning has taken into consideration the laying out of streets, business centers, residential areas, public buildings, accessibility of schools, with the practical purpose of public convenience, and to provide greater comfort at less cost to home owners.

6722 Hammerstone Way
Job 138
1951

6718 Hammerstone Way – Mariemont   Job 156-D
1951

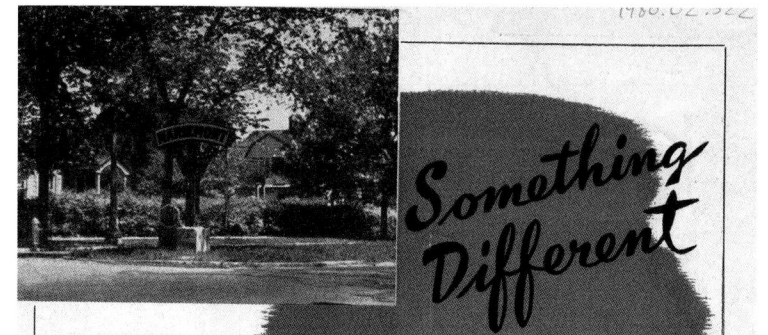

Something Different

THE MODEL TOWN OF MARIEMONT
A Town PLANNED for Gracious Living

Live in a Town of NATIONAL RENOWN . . .

The Town of Mariemont has so many advantages to home owners that it has achieved national renown as a residential section unsurpassed in the entire country.

Four hundred and fifty acres purchased in 1920 for the sole purpose of establishing a conveniently located residential community is now a reality.

Today, dreams of the founders of Mariemont have come true. Here are exceptional advantages to be considered: location accessible to all suburbs including the center of Cincinnati, transportation (bus lines direct to city), business centers, municipal improvements, Centralized heat, all utility services underground, recreational building, parks and playgrounds, public school system unsurpassed, churches, Mariemont Hospital, Mariemont Inn, quietude and comfort, safeguarding restrictions, insured land policy with each purchase. Remember, too, that land prices are below average level of other sections, shorn of Mariemont advantages.

MARIEMONT . . .
where it is . . .

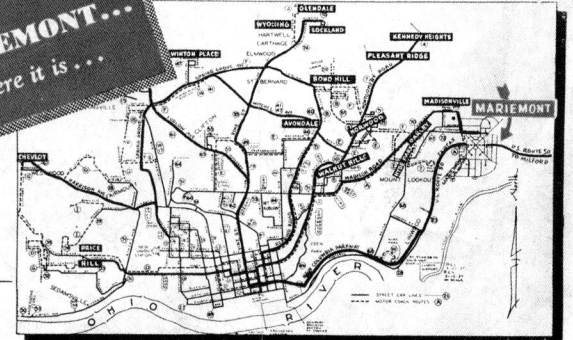

Entering the Twenty-First Century: 1960 and Beyond

Today and the Future

Mariemont's genesis depended on three individuals. Together they fashioned a community in the 1920s that had few peers and was, as Nolen's 1921 plan labeled it, a "National Exemplar" of town planning. The triumvirate hoped that similar planned communities would "be prosecuted with like energy into an indefinite future and carried to great consummation . . . replanned for the new day and architecturally worthy of all," as Nolen stated.

What did Mariemont accomplish?

A planned community that retained the integrity of its plan.

Housing for both renters and owners in a suburban setting.

Revival architectural styles and retention of them.

Saving of woods, streams, bluffs, and other natural features.

Creation of a walkable "streetscape" from end to end.

Integration of residential, commercial, educational, and recreational facilities.

Placement of utilities below ground for aesthetic purposes.

Establishment of a set-aside industrial section.

Placement of schools within walking distance of every part of the village.

Planned deed restrictions and building code to accommodate and support the Nolen plan.

What are Mariemont's lessons locally and nationally?

The extensive bibliography on Nolen and Mariemont might well be studied for ideas and concepts to be employed elsewhere.

Planning a community is better than letting one evolve without a plan.

Aesthetic principles should be studied so that they benefit human needs.

Resident satisfaction in livability should be aimed for in all its meanings.

Citizens should be encouraged to be caretakers and promoters of the Mariemont vision.

On a sunny day in 1971, swirling through the air on a carousel was popular entertainment for children at Mariemont's Ice Cream Social, held at Dogwood Park. Originally called the May Festival and held on the church lawn when it began in 1930, the Ice Cream Social ended in the 1980s.

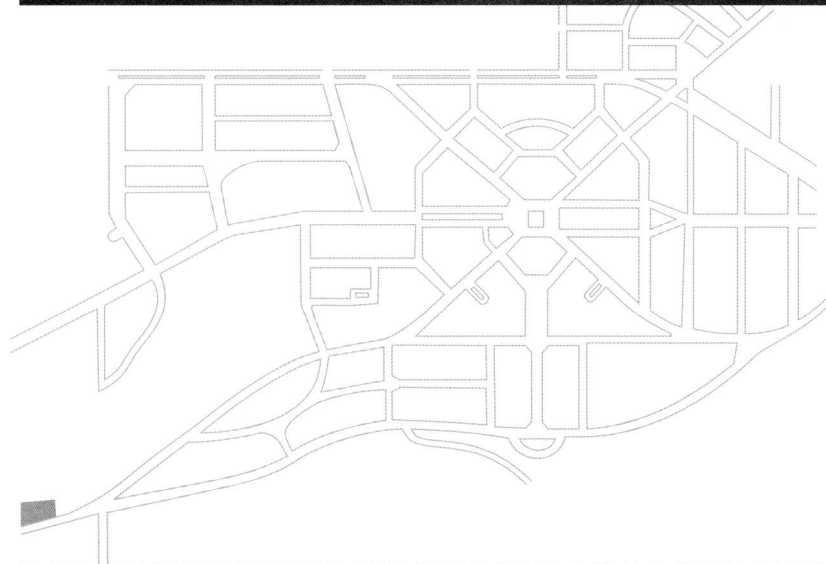

Swimming in Mariemont's outdoor pools is a vast improvement over running through the sprinklers set up on Mariemont's streets in the 1920s by the fire department! At the far western end of Mariemont Avenue, just above Whiskey Creek and surrounded by woods, is the Mariemont Swim Club, providing facilities for swimmers in its two pools. This location utilizes a portion of the Madisonville Site. The pools have been improved several times since the facility was initiated in 1957, with the pools and clubhouse undergoing renovation in 1989.

1800   1900   1910   1920   1930   1940

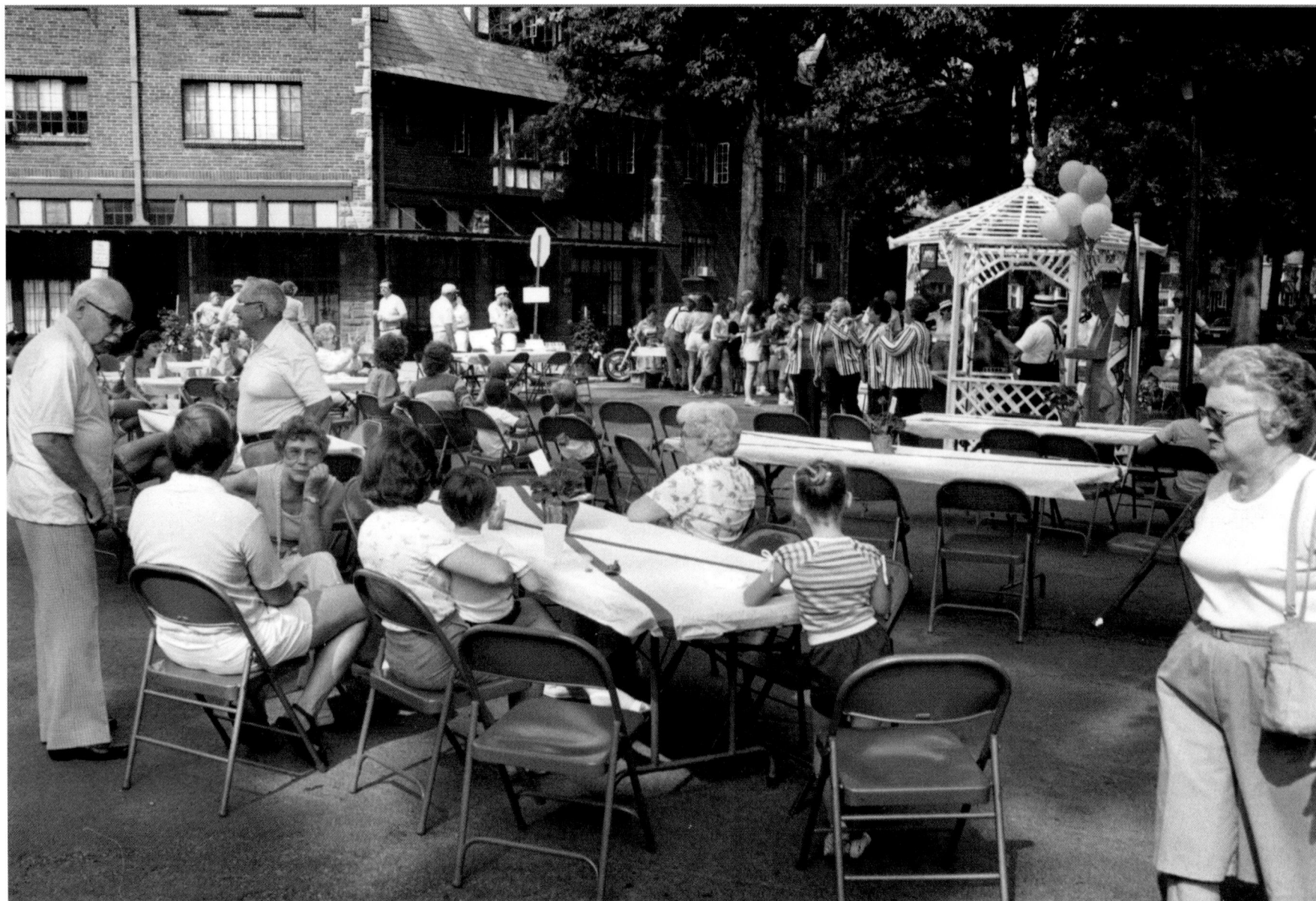

By 1984, the Ice Cream Social had moved to the old town square, at the intersection of Oak and Chestnut Streets, where entertainment focused on the gazebo.

1800   1900   1910   1920   1930   1940

Some might say that Mariemont is a village of anachronisms, with its quaint appearance as an English country town, its stone church with medieval roof emulating parish churches of the fourteenth century, and Tudor Revival architecture evoking the time of Henry VIII. Mariemont even has a town crier, an elected office established about the time of incorporation in 1941. Long ago in Great Britain and in our American colonies, town criers were popular, even necessary, dispensers of news and laws.

Today, Mariemont's town crier attends and opens all major political and festive events. Wearing his handsome period costume with tricornered hat, long coat, and waistcoat, he rings his bell to summon all to hear his greetings. Past town criers include Andy Anderson, Floyd Miller, Maurice LeBosquet, Bob Taylor, and Ralph Smith (shown at left).

Hank Kleinfeldt is the current office holder.

Until the Mariemont Inn began construction in 1925, the borders of the town square were vacant and unenclosed, with the exception of the beech grove at the square's eastern edge,. In 1938, development began to fill the north side of the town square with a movie theater and six stores. Early occupants included Horton's Drug Store and Central Trust Bank.

Shops and stores in the ground level of the paired Ripley and LeBoutillier apartment buildings bordering the old town square served as the shopping center for residents of Mariemont after 1925. This center included a Kroger grocery until 1927, when it moved to Oak Street, then in 1941 to Madisonville Road and Wooster Pike, by 1952 to the corner of Wooster Pike and West Street, and finally east of town to Columbia Township.

VILLAGE OF MARIEMONT

National Historic Landmark
2007
National Park Service
U.S. Department of the Interior

In 2007, Mariemont was designated by the United States Department of the Interior as a National Historic Landmark, the highest honor for sites, buildings, communities, and other historic entities of national importance. For several years previously, Mariemont was listed on the National Register of Historic Places.

VILLAGE OF MARIEMONT

THE VISION OF MARY M. EMERY AND
DESIGN OF TOWN PLANNER JOHN NOLEN

HAS BEEN DESIGNATED A

NATIONAL HISTORIC LANDMARK

THIS SITE POSSESSES NATIONAL SIGNIFICANCE
IN COMMEMORATING THE HISTORY OF THE
UNITED STATES OF AMERICA

2007

NATIONAL PARK SERVICE
UNITED STATES DEPARTMENT OF THE INTERIOR

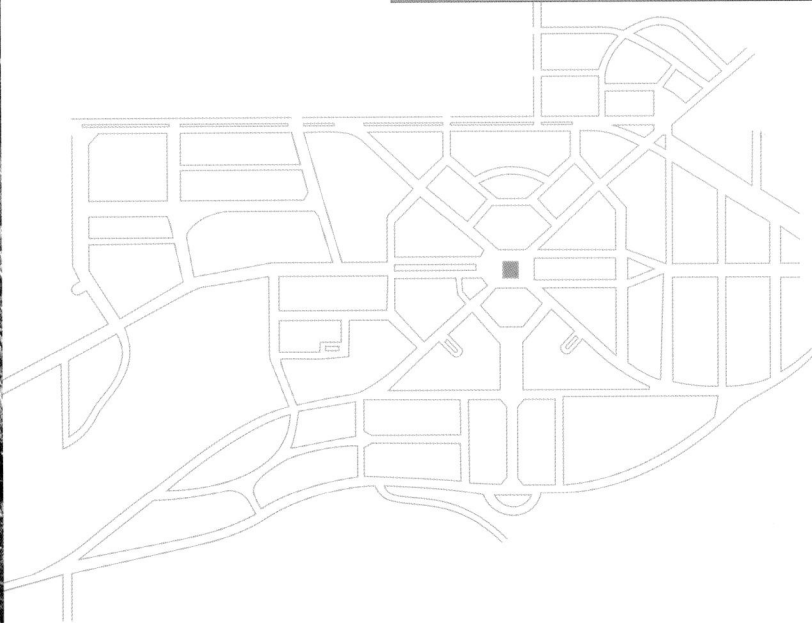

1980

1990

2000

147

An ice cream cone or sundae at Graeter's is a gustatory event never forgotten. Graeter's had its beginnings in Horton's Drug Store in 1946 and moved to its present location at the corner of Miami Road and Wooster Pike in the 1960s. The shop, in its Georgian-style building topped by a cupola, is a notable icon and destination in Mariemont.

This building that stretches along Madisonville Road near the town square today houses U.S. Bank, the Villager, and Mio's Restaurant in red brick and stone fronts with slightly Tudor-style trim. For twenty-three years, a branch library of the Cincinnati and Hamilton County system preceded this group, serving as the Mariemont public library. In 1971, ground was broken for a new facility that was built at the corner of Pocahontas and Wooster Pike.

Today and the Future

Originally, Mariemont's plan placed an elaborate arcaded, three-story structure on the north side of the town square. This imagined building never emerged far beyond the drawing board of Cincinnati architects Joseph Steinkamp and Brother.

Today, the complex includes PNC Bank, the Mariemont Theatre, the Quarter restaurant, and Graeter's ice cream and baked goods shop.

1800   1900   1910   1920   1930   1940

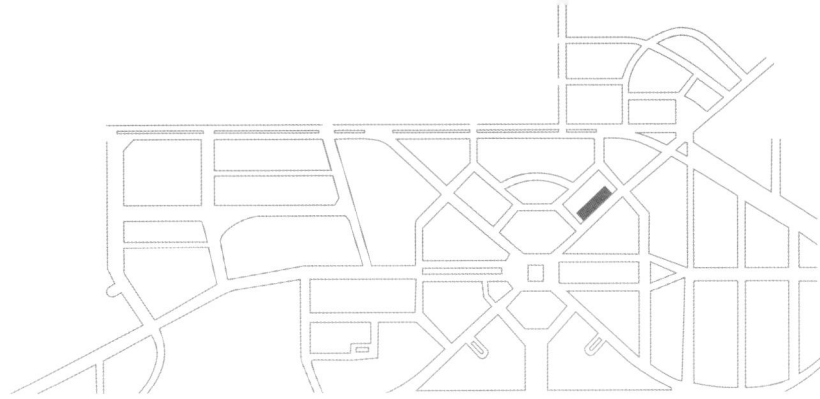

The largest new residential project in Mariemont since the formative days in the 1920s is Jordan Park, a condominium development of twenty-six units that opened in 2008 on Miami Road near the town square. Its architecture sensitively repeats the persistent style prevalent in the community and overlooks the dense woods of E. Boyd Jordan Memorial Park.

Near the Mary M. Emery Carillon and Mariemont's Tot Lot on Pleasant Street near Wooster Pike is the Clarence Erickson Shelter, overlooking the playing fields of Dogwood Park. The structure commemorates Mayor Erickson's many years of service to the village.

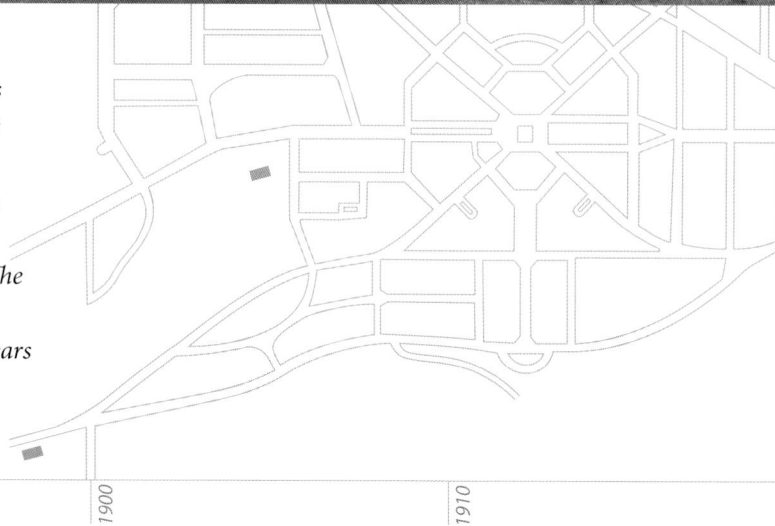

At the Madisonville Site in the 1920s, the Mariemont Company intended to build the "Indian Museum" as an outdoor facility to "display behind strong plate glass the finds that are constantly being made of skeletons and Indian relics which have made the 'station' near Madisonville, Ohio, world-famous," as

the Mariemont Company's promotional brochure (1925) indicated. Designed by John Nolen, the museum was never built at that time. Fortunately, Nolen's elevation drawings remained available. From these, the open-air building was constructed in the area as Nolen proposed but minus the display of any

objects or remains of the Native American culture that once occupied the bluff and surrounding area. In 2001, the Mariemont Preservation Foundation dedicated the John Nolen Pavilion as part of its 75th Anniversary Commemorative and Renewal Project.

1800   1900   1910   1920   1930   1940

Today and the Future

Hedges, brick walkway, and picket fence blend in this shaded view of the whitewashed walls of residences on Albert Place.

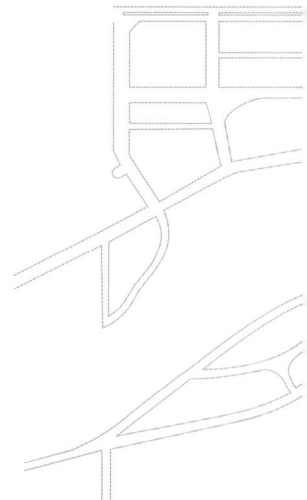

1800   1900   1910   1920   1930   1940

Many residential streets were planned with no curbs, while many were bordered by curbs of cut granite, especially at the intersections. Nolen and Livingood sought the informal appearance of an English country village, with wandering lanes, no curbs, and a cover of shade trees, as shown in this view of Sheldon Close.

Throughout Mariemont are many hidden corners and open vistas delighting residents and visitors, offering attractive vignettes such as the metal gates leading to the Carillon.

Today and the Future

A comfortable resting spot at the old town square at the intersection of Oak and Chestnut Streets is enhanced by the attractive garden and bubbling fountain.

Shadows dance across the houses designed by Charles W. Short on Oak Street.

Because the Mariemont Strand, with its steeply pitched roof, half-timber and stucco, and gables, so closely resembles its near neighbor, the Mariemont Inn, many visitors think it was among the buildings originally planned and built by the Mariemont Company in the 1920s. However, it was constructed in 1992 on the old site of the Kroger store on Wooster Pike. This commercial building's owner and architect were sensitive to the character of the village as plotted in 1921.

Outdoor dining has existed in Mariemont since its beginnings, when the Mariemont Inn provided "a delightful retreat from the heat of the city" in its summer garden at the rear of the Inn, where the parking lot now exists. Today, the National Exemplar restaurant in the Inn and other eating establishments, provide popular outdoor dining on Wooster Pike and clustered on or near the town square.

Traffic, both pedestrian and automotive, circulates around the town square. At its center, the fountain encourages reflecting on Mariemont's ambience with views into a thick woods of beech trees, attractive shops, restaurants, the Inn, a movie theater, and the radiating streets seen from this center point.

A close look at the fountain's base and pedestal reveals bunches of daffodils, the official flower of Mariemont, with the bowls formed by leaves and topped by a budding daffodil flower. The fountain was designed by Mariemont resident Karen Monzel in 1991 for the 50th Anniversary celebration of the incorporation of Mariemont.

A Contemporary View of Mariemont: 2000-2010

Robert Flischel, Photographer

Robert Flischel graduated from Xavier University in 1971. He studied photography under Kazik Pazovski and credits his own clean, direct style to Pazovski's influence. Mr. Flischel is a founding trustee of Radio Reading Service, which assists the visually impaired. He has served on the Board of the regional chapter of the American Society of Media Photographers and is President Emeritus of the Art League of Cincinnati. Mr. Flischel has taught photography at Northern Kentucky University and lectures frequently on historic preservation.

His photography books include *The University of Cincinnati: Architectural Transformation* (RAF Press, 2007); *Cincinnati Illuminated: A Photographic Journal* (RAF Press, 2003); *An Expression of the Community: Cincinnati Public Schools' Legacy of Art and Architecture* (Art League Press, 2001); *New Bremen 2000* (Orange Frazer Press, 2000); *Then and Now: Cincinnati and Northern Kentucky* (Scripps Howard, 1995); and *Perspectives, Cincinnati: The Towers Perrin Collection* (Robert A. Flischel / Towers Perrin, 1993).

Robert Flischel's photographs have appeared in *Life Magazine*, *Time*, *BusinessWeek*, *Town and Country*, *Newsweek*, *Audubon Magazine*, *Smithsonian Magazine*, *Ohio Magazine*, *Cincinnati Magazine*, and many others.

Mr. Flischel has been a contributing photographer to many books, including *Cincinnati: The Queen City; Building Ohio: A Traveler's Guide to Ohio's Urban Architecture* (Orange Frazer Press, 2001); and *Tall Stacks: A Celebration of America's Steamboat Heritage* (Wolfe, 1995).

It is generally conceded that no other American town is so complete or so perfect from the garden city or garden suburb point of view.

John Nolen
("*Mariemont, Ohio—A New Town Built to Produce Local Happiness,*" American Civic Annual 1 *[1929]: 236*)

Robert Flischel, Photographer

To the youth of Mariemont, in memory of its founder, my beloved sister, Mary Muhlenberg Emery, A.D. 1929 [inscribed on "Bourdon," the largest bell in the Mariemont Carillon].

Isabella F. Hopkins

(quotation inscribed on "Bourdon," the largest bell in the Mariemont Carillon)

Mariemont stands out as the most worthwhile project on which I had the privilege of being professionally involved.

John Nolen

(letter to Charles J. Livingood, May 9, 1932, Nolen Collection, Cornell University)

Robert Flischel, Photographer

Is the sun a little brighter there in Mariemont?

Is the air a little fresher?

Is your house a little sweeter? Is your housework somewhat easier?

And the children, do you feel safer about them?

Are their faces a bit ruddier, are their legs a little sturdier?

Do they laugh and play a lot louder in Mariemont?

Then I am content.

Mary M. Emery
(Mariemont Messenger, *March 19, 1926*)

The town plan of Mariemont had a reverence for the site on which the town was to be built, and reflected in all its physical aspects the physical factors of the topography and of the controlling elements of circulation in the surrounding territory.

John Nolen

(A Descriptive and Pictured Story of Mariemont—A New Town: "A National Exemplar" [Cincinnati: Mariemont Company, 1925], page 41)

To have an object of unceasing pleasure—of course that is what Mariemont represents and therefore I must be in a condition of bliss!

Mary M. Emery

(letter to John Nolen, October 5, 1923, Nolen Collection, Cornell University)

Robert Flischel, Photographer

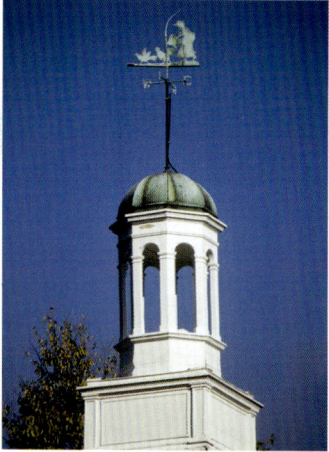

Mariemont is not a philanthropy or in any way paternalistic. Its sponsor, Mrs. Mary M. Emery, herself a lifelong resident of Cincinnati, is simply showing in a very practical way her interest in proper development of home life and home ownership by providing an ideal place for home building.

Charles J. Livingood

(A Descriptive and Pictured Story of Mariemont—A New Town: *"A National Exemplar"* [Cincinnati: Mariemont Company, 1925], page ii)

1800   1900   1910   1920   1930   1940

Village Square, March 6, 1931

Early view (ca. 1925) from the northeast corner of Mariemont, showing a section of Resthaven Barn (building with cupola, lower right) and Dale Park School (brick building with cupola, upper center) and surrounding neighborhood.

Construction of Maple Street houses, October 14, 1924.

176

Designed and typeset by Karen Monzel Hughes using Gill Sans Light and Minion Italic.

Gill Sans was designed by Eric Gill and was released in 1928 by Monotype Corporation. Gill had worked with Edward Johnston on his typeface for the London Underground, and Gill Sans took its inspiration from that font. Gill's intent was to design the ultimate legible sans-serif text face, to function equally well for text and display usage.

Minion was designed by Robert Slimbach in 1990 for Adobe Systems, inspired by late Renaissance-era type. The name derives from the traditional naming system for type sizes, in which minion is between nonpareil and brevier.

Printed by Kings Time Printing Press, Ltd., on 140 gsm China Gold East Matte Coated art paper.

Smyth sewn case binding by Kings Time Printing Press, Ltd., with Brillianta premium cloth over 3mm case boards.